Kings & Kingdoms

Anointing a New Generation of Kings to Serve the King of Kings

BEN R. PETERS

Kings and Kingdoms
© 2009 by Ben R. Peters

Published by
OPEN HEART MINISTRIES
15648 Bombay Blvd.
S. Beloit, IL 61080
www.ohmint.org
benrpeters@juno.com

ISBN: 978-0-9789884-3-2

Cover image © 2008 by João Lourenço
Cover design and book interior by *www.ChristianBookDesign.com*

CONTENTS

PREFACE

Very few people today have first-hand knowledge of what it means to live as a subject of an earthly king in the way that most people did who lived during Bible times. The biblical references to kings and kingdoms were well understood in those days. Those of us who live in democratic societies probably miss a good deal of the implications of the kingdom references in the Bible.

When John, the Beloved, wrote that Jesus has made us kings and priests unto God, he was making a powerful statement. And when Jesus is called a King of kings, the people knew very well what that meant.

Like most of my readers, I have no experience in being a part of an earthly kingdom. But God in his mercy and eternal purpose has blessed me with some revelation designed to "energize His base" on the earth. That revelation relates to what it means to be a king under a greater king. Stay with me on this journey to discover who you really are and how you can truly "seek first the Kingdom of God" by fulfilling your role as a king over your part of His Kingdom.

NOTE: The topic is about kings, but sometimes the monarch is a female – a queen. The exact same principles will apply. At this point, it should be clarified that it's not a male function being discussed. It's for both men and women of God who take the call of God seriously.

CHAPTER ONE

KING SAUL IS DYING

*T*he archers have sent their arrows and King Saul is severely wounded. He's not dead yet, but his time is short, and David is waiting in the wings. It's time to get excited about a new day in the Kingdom of Heaven on this old earth.

Desiring something fresh from God, I opened my Bible before speaking at a conference. My eyes fell on I Samuel 31:3, *"The battle became fierce against Saul. The archers hit him, and he was severely wounded by the archers."*

The Holy Spirit spoke immediately to me, *"The spirit of Saul is being taken out and the spirit of David is about to become the ruling spirit in my Kingdom."* Over the next several days, God downloaded one nugget of truth after another until I was bursting with this pregnant word.

The first and strongest message from this word was that many "Davids" are going to be released into their destiny, because many "Sauls", who have been holding on to their positions and titles, are being removed from their thrones. This is actually not so much about the "Davids" and "Sauls", but about the citizens of the Kingdom that they impact, and the billion souls who will come into the Kingdom when God's power and authority are released through the "Davids".

These "Davids" are first and foremost worshipers. They are intimate lovers of Jesus. They have paid a price to know Him and truly love Him. They love God more than position, power or financial blessing. They are those that God can trust with spiritual authority. They will shortly take their place in major leadership positions in the Kingdom of Heaven on the earth.

THE SAUL SYNDROME

The problem with Saul was that he was another Ishmael – the result of man's ideas, not God's. The people wanted a king like all the other nations. God chose a man who would please them, a man head and shoulders taller than any of the others. He gave them a leader they could respect who was not just a priest, like Samuel, but a leader for their armies. It gave them a sense of security to have someone they could see and admire.

But clearly, Saul was not prepared for the pressures of the Kingdom. The desires of the people put him in a place he was not capable of handling. In like manner, many Christian leaders have been put into positions by the good ideas of men rather than the wisdom and counsel of the Lord because they looked like good leaders. The problem is that neither the people nor the leaders they exalt have learned to hear God's voice. Instead, they function on natural wisdom and strategy.

When young "Davids" arise and get too much attention, the "Sauls" get fearful of losing their authority, honor and power. They refuse to empower them lest the people sing, "Saul has slain his thousands, but David his ten thousands." Once a "Saul" has climbed the ladder of success, the thought of a "David" climbing above them and potentially replacing them is hard to handle.

"Sauls" Lack of Vision

Saul totally missed the potential of being a loving "papa" to David by not empowering him to fulfill his destiny as a mighty warrior and subsequent ruler in the Kingdom. Had Saul given David free reign, like Pharaoh had done for Joseph, Saul would have lived a very good life in peace and prosperity.

Instead, Saul spent incredible resources hunting David to take his life, while his Kingdom remained in poverty and oppressed by the Philistines. David had defeated the Philistines many times when he had led Saul's armies.

For instance, when David was fleeing from Saul, he fled to the caves near the Dead Sea at En Gedi, at the eastern edge of Israel. When Saul heard about this, he took his army and headed east to capture and kill David. Meanwhile, on the western border of Israel, the Philistines attacked the unprotected nation. Saul had to quickly abandon his compelling desire to kill David and turn his attention to the invaders on his western border.

It is obvious that seeking David's life was detrimental to Saul and the nation of Israel in two ways:

1. First of all, Saul was wasting energy and resources chasing David, and the Philistines were able to take advantage of his preoccupation with David.
2. Secondly, Saul was not taking advantage of David's amazing abilities to wage war.

Ultimately, Saul's premature death and the death of his son, Jonathan, were the result of Saul's fear and lack of vision as to what David could have done for him. Saul had nothing to fear from him. David proved that twice later when he was advised to kill Saul and had tremendous opportunity to do so. But, of course, David refused to strike God's anointed king. But, as we shared above, in chasing David, Saul left an open door for the Philistines to strike Israel. In the end, that open door cost him his life.

Had Saul let David run his military operations, David would have subdued all Saul's enemies, which he did do later when he became the king. When David ruled over all of Israel, he brought all the surrounding nations under his control. They had to pay tribute to David, making him an incredibly wealthy king. David could have done the same for King Saul and preserved his life at the same time.

If Saul had listened to God, he might have made David king while he was still alive, like David did for Solomon. If he had been willing to decrease and to let David increase, he would have been remembered as a great leader instead of a demonized, foolish king.

Saul's Impatience

Like the Israelites who were impatient to have a king, Saul revealed his own impatience in a crucial test of his kingship. Saul had little history in seeking God, and he was not a friend of God like David was. When he became fearful, he got religious and offered the sacrifices that only Samuel was authorized to do. He couldn't wait *for* God because he had never learned to wait *on* God. His impatience cost him his kingdom.

What is interesting is the fact that Saul had been anointed by Samuel, not only to be king, but also to prophesy. Sometimes we think that if we only had a powerful spiritual gift, we would be awesome for God. But it wasn't enough to keep Saul from destruction and it's not enough for us either.

The Saul spirit within us wants us to get religious and do religious things rather than simply wait on God and trust in God. Patience is a result of deep-seated trust, coming from lots of experience in waiting on God.

SAUL'S FEAR

When Saul was still small in his own eyes, God exalted him. But when he was exalted, without a strong and intimate relationship with God, he became fearful that someone like David would remove him from his exalted throne. Saul became paranoid and controlling to protect his position and power. He even had a monument made in his name. He thus opened himself up to so much demonic oppression, anger and hatred that he tried to kill both David and his own son, Jonathan.

Believe it or not, there are a lot of ministers and ministries who have in many ways become like King Saul. They hold on to their exalted place, even when the anointing has moved on to another man or woman.

THE DAVID MANTLE

David was a different story. David was God's choice, not man's. Even Samuel would not have chosen David. God had to give Samuel a little lecture about how He looked at people when He was choosing a leader. Eliab, David's eldest brother, had an imposing outward appearance like Saul, but God told Samuel not to look at the outward appearance, but at the heart.

David was also the youngest, his father didn't even consider him worthy of a shot at the position of king, and he was treated with disdain by his older brothers. Having grown up with two older brothers, I know what it feels like to be the "little kid". No one really respects you or wants to hear what you have to say. I can't imagine having seven older brothers telling me what to do or telling me to "get lost", etc.

However, David turned that rejection to his own advantage. He found "Someone" that did want to listen to him, so he spent a lot of time writing songs and singing to God, accompanying himself on the harp. David became familiar with the presence of God, when no one was around but his sheep.

David did not focus on the rejection he felt from his family, but on the One who was always there for him. He became a worshiper and built his faith through intimacy with God. The result was that he became a warrior and killed a lion and a bear with his hands. Later, he would kill Goliath, even after his brothers scolded him for coming to the battlefield. David was being prepared for his future role as king of Israel. It was not the training method that man would have chosen, but God knew what He was doing.

I believe that God did want to give Israel a king, because Jesus was to fulfill the triple role of prophet, priest and king. The prophet who preceded Jesus was Moses, the priest was Melchizedek, and the King was David. But David, God's choice, had to go into hiding because man's choice stayed in power when he should have turned over the Kingdom to God's choice.

David did not operate in his own wisdom. He constantly sought the Lord when making decisions. If he won a battle a certain way the first time, he didn't assume that he could win the next battle the same way. He sought the Lord for wisdom with each battle, and God gave him a new strategy every time.

This came naturally to David because he was a friend of God. He was a worshiper first, a warrior second and a king third. When he did sin and offended God, he was desperate for his relationship to be restored as we read in Psalm 51. Saul, on the other hand, wanted his kingdom and honor to be maintained at all costs. His relationship with God was shallow and not strong enough when the pressure came. Even after God had rejected him, Saul still wanted Samuel to honor him in front of the people.

Today, many "Davids" are being raised up in a multitude of ministries and settings, both in the western world and in the developing nations. The persecuted church is also producing many passionate lovers and worshipers that God will unleash at just the right time. Houses of prayer are inspiring and raising up a multitude of worshipers whom God will entrust with unprecedented power, authority and financial resources for the harvest.

It May Come in Stages

As you read the story of David, you become aware that he was not anointed just once, he was anointed three times. The first time was by Samuel when he was seventeen. It would still be many years before he took the throne, but he knew God's hand was on him, and he had the patience to wait for his destiny. The second time, he was anointed by the elders of Judah, and he reigned over his own tribe for a couple of years. It was a great honor, but it was not everything God had for him. The house of Saul was still in charge of the rest of Israel, but we read that Saul's house got weaker and David got stronger. Finally, David was anointed by all the elders of Israel, and he was able to complete his full destiny.

You may find yourself somewhere on this journey. If God has given you the vision and the dream, hold on to it. If God has given you a throne at a certain level of fulfillment, don't settle for less than God's best for you. Be faithful, but not complacent with where you are. Keep asking God for more. After David was made king of all Israel, he expanded his kingdom even further. The nations around him became his servants and the source of great revenue.

WORSHIPERS RULE

In the next few years, God will release a greater glory on the church than we have ever seen. What happened in Lakeland, Florida, was a genuine foretaste of what is coming, despite the fact that the leader of the outpouring was unable to handle his fleshly weaknesses. The reality of the presence of God in that place, His power and His love were overpowering to all who attended with an open mind and heart.

At the same time, God is beginning to release an incredible transfer of wealth for the Kingdom. This has been delayed because of the lack of preparation in the church. There has been too much of a Saul spirit in the church, and that spirit would misuse and abuse the glory and wealth. But the Saul spirit is dying, and the spirit of David, the worshiper/warrior, is arising to take the throne of leadership in the Kingdom of Heaven on the earth.

The result will be the "Golden Age" of the church, just as the Kingdoms of David and Solomon were called the "Golden Age" of Israel. In this age, the world will honor, respect and bless the Kingdom of Heaven and will come to believe in the one true God who loves them and has given His children such glory.

But the turning point is the transfer of spiritual authority from the "Sauls" to the "Davids", and this is what God is waiting for. He can't bless what is still under the control of the Saul spirit, but He will abundantly bless the spirit of David on the earth.

I suspect that within most of us there is a mixture of Saul and David. If we want power and authority that we can handle, we need to kill the Saul spirit and empower the David spirit within us.

We all need to pursue the heart of David, the worshiper/warrior. We can and should all become true worshipers, worshiping our Father in Heaven and His Son, Jesus Christ, in spirit and truth. The word of the Lord that came to me is very clear – *worshipers will rule.*

EXTREME MAKEOVER COMING

The church of tomorrow will look quite different from the church of today. The outbreak of miraculous power through the lives and testimonies of ecclesiastical nobody's will shift the loyalty of both old and new Christians from the established leaders to those who have not only the word, but the power of God. (I Cor. 4:19, 20)

Christian leaders who humble themselves and embrace the revival will continue to provide guidance and pastoral care. But those who react like Saul in irrational jealousy will lose their place of honor and be vulnerable to the arrows of the enemy. They will become tormented in relationships, finances and health.

Nothing will calm their spirit except the "Davids" who play the harp for them. This relief will only be temporary unless they repent and release their position to the "Davids" among them. They may fight to hold onto power and honor, but they will eventually fall without the protection of the Lord.

Worshipers rejoice! Your day is coming! You may be wondering when you will be released into your destiny. Have patience! Don't embrace the spirit of impatience from Saul. Keep worshiping! Keep warring for God! Exalt the name of Jesus! Get to know Him while you care for a few sheep. Get to know Him when the "Goliaths" present themselves. Get to know Him in the caves when you are hiding from Saul.

Don't try to kill Saul yourself. He was anointed by Samuel, just like you. He may not respect your anointing, but you must respect his. Serve him as much as you can, but wait for God's timing when you want to fight back. He is in control and your day will come. Until then, discover what David learned – that God is your refuge and strength and a very present help in time of need.

Long Live King David!

Today, God is speaking to His church that there are kingdoms that need kings to rule and reign in righteousness and truth. He is preparing us to sit on thrones with Him and govern His land, but there is certainly some special preparation needed for this. In the next chapter, we'll learn some very important truths to prepare us for this high calling.

Chapter Two

Accepting Our Roles as Kings

We've often said that churches and other ministries should be busy building the Kingdom of God and not their own little kingdoms. There is some truth to that statement, but I now realize there is also a problem with it.

Revelation 1:6 declares that Jesus has made us to become kings and priests unto God. How can we be kings unless we have a kingdom to rule over? Without a kingdom to rule, the title "king" is meaningless. But how does that work in the light of our tendency to love the honor what comes from man?

On one hand, we want to maintain humility and smallness in our own eyes. On the other hand, we tend to become corrupted by too much power and wealth. Clearly, we must get God's perspective and avoid the ditch on both sides of the road on this issue.

Ditch # 1: The Pride of Power

It is true that many people, like King Saul, do build their own little kingdoms for their own selfish purposes. They love the honor and power they receive by being at the top of their mountain – the king of their own kingdom. Their pride is in full bloom, and they often suffer disastrous falls from their high perch. Truly, this is not what we need to emulate in our own lives.

Ditch # 2: False Humility – Rejecting Kingly Assignments

Others have accepted lies from the adversary that they are not worthy to be in positions of authority and power. They never fulfill their call to be kings and priests unto God. This may seem like humility, but it is a false humility, based on the lies of the enemy. These people not only miss out on the opportunity to be used mightily by God, but they also rob God of the opportunity to expand His wonderful Kingdom through them.

The High and Holy Pathway – Kings and Kingdoms Under the Authority of the King of Kings and His Glorious Kingdom

It is frankly ridiculous to say we are to be kings without a kingdom to rule. A king without a kingdom is only a king in his own mind. When God calls us kings, He clearly is saying that we are to rule over a kingdom. If someone says he is a leader but no one is following him, is he fulfilling his role as a leader? Surely, the same principle applies to kings and kingdoms. To fulfill our role as kings, God gives us a kingdom to administrate for Him.

However, we have little understanding today of what it means to be a king under the King of Kings. People in biblical times understood this because of their culture. There were, of course, times when kings were sovereign over a geographical area without any earthly king ruling over them, but the greater portion of both biblical and secular history tells a different story.

Most kings ruled at the permission of a greater king. The term, "king of kings", is used six times in Scripture – three times in the Old Testament and three times in the New Testament. The three New Testament references all refer to Jesus as the King of Kings (I Tim. 6:15, Rev. 17:14, 19:16), but the three in the Old Testament refer to earthly emperors. Two of these references refer to Nebuchadnezzar of Babylon (Eze. 26:7, Dan. 2:37), and the other refers to Artaxerxes, king over the Persian Empire (Ezr. 7:12).

EMPORERS RULE

The emperor was a king over other kings who ruled at his pleasure. These "underling" kings had a certain amount of power, but could be replaced or killed by the higher king. Such was King Herod over Israel, under Rome, at the time of the birth of Jesus. He had power to make decrees and raise taxes, etc., as long as he pleased the Caesar in Rome.

Even David and Solomon were kings over other kings, although their empires did not stretch far beyond their immediate neighbors. Nonetheless, the nations around them were forced to submit to the rule of these two powerful monarchs.

A quick look at world history, after Israel's golden days under David and Solomon, reveals that emperors ruled the then-known world for many centuries. The great Assyrian Empire, which conquered the northern tribes of Israel, was followed by the Babylonian Empire, which conquered Judah, along with most of the then-known world.

The Babylonian Empire was overthrown by the Medes and Persians. Alexander the Great then conquered the world for Greece. Finally, Julius Caesar of Rome conquered the Greeks, and the mighty Roman Empire ruled the world with an iron fist for many centuries.

Most nations never knew what it meant to be a sovereign nation for a millennium or longer. Before the Roman Empire began, Israel almost attained a 100-year period (164 BC to 63 BC) of independence courtesy of the Maccabees, who staged a revolt against the Greeks. It would then be over two thousand years before Israel would once again become a truly sovereign nation in 1948. Even now, Israel must cooperate somewhat with America and the United Nations to survive, clearly diminishing their own sovereignty.

The point being made is that most people in the world today have had no experience living under the direct rule of a sovereign king in their own nation. They often have had kings over them, but these kings were under the sovereign rule of a "king of kings". To them, a king in their own land was only an administrator for the king of kings in Babylon, Greece or Rome.

THE KING OF KINGS NEEDS SERVANT KINGS
TO ADMINISTRATE HIS MEGA-KINGDOM

Kings who ruled under the authority of a "king of kings" fulfilled an important role in the administration of the "mega-kingdom". No one man could control so many nations without a lot of regional help. He would give the position of king or governor to someone who would do his bidding and keep the people in line.

These subservient kings gave their subjects the feeling that someone of their own nation was their king, and it kept the anger and resentment down at the thought of being under a foreign king. For this and other practical reasons, it was to the advantage of the king of kings to have these servant kings in place, taking care of the needs of their own people.

THE MORE KINGS UNDER THE KING OF KINGS, THE MORE HONOR HE RECEIVED

A king over two or three other kings would have some honor, but a king over hundreds of foreign kings would be given incredible honor and respect. He would be seen as all powerful and to be greatly feared. No one could commit a crime against the king and then escape to another country, because the king ruled over every nation.

In like manner, having many kings under Jesus, the King of all Kings, does not diminish His authority – it increases it. Therefore, in a very real way, the sooner we all comprehend that we are called to be kings under our King of Kings, the sooner we can fulfill Matthew 6:33, which tells us to "Seek first the Kingdom of God."

We enlarge the Kingdom of God when we accept our roles as kings and as we subsequently build up more kings and their kingdoms. However, we must be totally submitted to the fact that we serve only for the pleasure of our King of Kings and not for our own pleasure. As kings, we have much responsibility and the authority to go along with it. We get to use the vast resources of our kingdom, but they all belong to the King of Kings when He wants them.

Responsibilities of Kings

First of all, we'll look at some of the responsibilities of a king. There are many, but we will highlight three of the most important ones. We will then look at the rights or privileges of being a king.

1. Justice

One of the greatest responsibilities of a ruler is to ensure that justice is carried out. Whoever is chosen to govern the people has the power to protect the people from being exploited, as well as the power to exploit them. Far too many rulers use this power to exploit their people for their own personal advantage, but God wants us to use this power to bring justice.

Solomon was an excellent example for us. He asked God for the wisdom to rule over the Israelites, but he acknowledged that they were not his people, but God's people. In gratitude to God for visiting him and promising him understanding, wisdom, wealth and honor, Solomon offered sacrifices of thanksgiving to God.

Solomon's very first duty as a king, after offering sacrifices to God, was to be a judge and to bring justice. Two women came to him with a very serious argument. One of their babies had died, and they both claimed the living child as their own. Solomon used the gift of wisdom to reveal who the real mother was.

Those called by God to be kings under the King of Kings should have justice high on their priority list. The Bible is full of references to the importance of bringing justice to the poor and defenseless. The church has done a reasonable job of this over the centuries, compared to secular governments, but the record is far from perfect.

Many ministries, in their rush to be the biggest and the best, have used their positions, platforms and charisma to exploit the poor in an attempt to take their ministries to a higher level of visibility and honor. Many ministries do great works of charity, but others may be taking more from the poor than they are giving back. They may justify this in a lot of different ways, but the results are not pleasing to the King of Kings whose eyes are always on the poor and the oppressed.

Frankly, it becomes very easy and very natural for those of us who are leaders in the Kingdom of God to court the friendship of the rich and the influential, while ignoring the needs of those who have little to offer us in return. Jesus severely chastised the religious leaders of His day for such behavior, and He would surely do it again today.

While it is true that leaders need to spend time working with other leaders for the sake of expanding the Kingdom, it is a very different matter to pursue relationships for personal advantage. God is very good at discerning our motives and He will judge fairly. He invites us to let Him help us judge our own hearts, so we don't have to be judged by Him in these matters.

Racial Justice

Recently I was sharing this concept with a men's group and without any plans to do so, I began to talk about injustice that we don't even realize exists. As white Americans, we often have an unconscious prejudice against other races living among us.

Obviously, from the way African Americans vote, they feel that the only way they will be given a fair shake is to have one of their own ruling the land. Hispanics are also a major minority in America, but are looked on as unwelcome guests by most Americans and treated with less respect because of their appearance, accent or cultural differences. Native Americans, also known as First Nations people, are another substantial group that have every right to live here, but don't always feel treated that way.

Millions of Asians also dwell among us, but because they have slightly different facial features, they carry a sense of not really belonging. They work hard to excel as professionals in medicine, business or law, just to be accepted in society. However, they never feel really equal with their western European equivalents. To some extent, the same thing holds true for Eastern Europeans, who have accents that betray that they are not born in America.

Justice May Mean Compensation for Past Injustice

I believe that true and biblical justice demands not only that everyone can use the same water fountains, bus seats and hotels, but that when we see that injustice has been done, we offer compensation for that injustice. This compensation does not have to be in huge monetary awards, but there should be at least some physical and tangible settlement that will have material and emotional value to show that we are truly sorry and sincerely desiring to heal the pain that we have caused in the past.

Whenever I have an appropriate opportunity, and I am prompted by the Holy Spirit, I apologize to groups or individuals of foreign origin for the way other Americans have treated them. It has often been a very emotional experience, and I have had Korean pastors confess that they have had attitudes toward

Americans because of other speakers who have come to Korea carrying and displaying a prideful spirit of superiority. They have shared that my apology to them was healing their hearts.

People from other nations and African Americans are a tremendous resource for America and the Kingdom of Heaven. We must not wait for our government to bring justice to them. Whoever shows them love and respect will win their hearts and their energy and strength. If the church does its job and leads the way in bringing them justice, we will win them for the Kingdom of Heaven. If we leave it up to the government, we will lose an incredible opportunity to expand the Kingdom of our King of Kings.

Thankfully, much is being done in these days to rectify the abuses of the past, but much more needs to be done. Our job is not finished until we feel comfortable with full integration and we make friends of those with different racial origins. Most of the Hispanics and others who are living in America, including those here illegally, are only here for economic survival. They would prefer to live in their own country if they could survive and provide for their families there. I have talked with many of them and they all agree. If we introduced them to our King of Kings and discipled them to become kings unto God, we could send them back to their own countries with our support to evangelize, pastor churches, and spread the gospel of the Kingdom in their own land among their own people. This is my idea of how to solve the illegal immigration problem.

Personal Perspective

I am extremely thankful to God for my Godly, missionary-hearted parents, who taught me to love all races. I am also extremely thankful for a man of God who invited me to Argentina, South America, in the fall of 1973. I was blessed to participate in an amazing six-week revival, where God's love and power were spectacular and flowing continuously. This immediately gave me a passionate love for the Spanish-speaking people, as well as their language. Worshiping in Spanish seemed more heavenly than worshiping in English.

I believe that anyone who had experienced what I did would soon have more love for other nationalities. I heartily endorse every Christian who is able to visit another country and also to minister to minorities in their own country. It changes your perspective completely.

Our Incredible Missions Opportunity

In America, we have the attitude that anyone coming to live in America should learn English if they want to be accepted. It is, of course, a good idea for their personal benefit. However, it's interesting to me that churches and denominations pay a lot of money to train missionaries and then send them to language school so that they can fulfill the Great Commission.

But what if God is bringing the mission field to our doorsteps? It's a lot cheaper for us to learn Spanish at home and begin to reach out to our Hispanic neighbors. What an opportunity God has given us! Are we throwing it away because we have no idea what God has in mind?

What if justice means that those who have had less opportunity to hear the gospel and to prosper financially in the past should be given the opportunity and privilege to compensate for their past injustice? Should we perhaps spend more of our time and money on evangelism and charity, even if it means some personal sacrifice?

2. PROTECTION

Another major responsibility of kings is to provide protection for all the people. It is also, of course, in his own self-interest to protect them, and not just to protect his own family and property. Without prosperous subjects to support his kingdom, he would not have a kingdom to rule over.

It's the king's responsibility to see that the armies are equipped and trained for battle. He must ensure that wise and courageous generals are overseeing the war plans and the strategies for national defense. He must be the Commander-in-Chief, even as our president is in America.

King Asa

The father of Jehoshaphat, King Asa, of Judah, was a very wise and godly king. II Chronicles 14 tells us that Asa had ten years of peace when he took over the throne. Asa wisely used this time to prepare for the inevitable battle that he knew would be coming. Neighboring nations were always trying to enlarge their borders, take plunder and/or subject another nation to their domination.

Asa built up the army, but also built walls, gates and towers in the cities of Judah. In addition, he cleansed the land of idolatry, so that God would not hold back His blessings from the land.

The inevitable finally took place, and a powerful foe camped on Judah's doorstep. It was the day that Asa had diligently prepared for. The Ethiopians with an army of a million strong, almost double the size of King Asa's army, attacked Judah. Asa had prepared well, but he knew that he still needed a miracle from God. We are told in Scripture that God fought for Israel, and they totally routed the Ethiopian army.

As they chased the fleeing soldiers, Judah also used the opportunity to take plunder from cities outside of their previous borders, and there was a great transfer of wealth from the neighboring cities to their own. All of this happened because King Asa knew it was his responsibility to provide protection and prepare for times of attack.

Kings in the Kingdom, who serve under the King of Kings, must also watch over the souls of their flocks, as instructed by Paul and Peter in various Scriptures. The enemy will often come as a wolf in sheep's clothing, and the king needs to set watchmen on the walls who can discern between the wolves and sheep.

Like Solomon, we need to acknowledge that the sheep we care for do not belong to us, no matter how much we have been honored and exalted. We are simply the under-shepherds who have the privilege and responsibility of taking care of His precious sheep.

And like King Asa, we should take advantage of whatever quiet time we can with God to prepare for the attack of the enemy. God will always give us that quiet time if we take advantage of it, so that we can build our defenses. These attacks would overwhelm us if we didn't have the confidence that God is with us and that we have done what we could to prepare. Then we can rest confidently in the supernatural power of God to protect and defend us and our sheep when the attacks come.

King David had been perfectly prepared for battle as he

cared for his sheep. During the times of loneliness, he found a friend in God and built his faith, as he worshiped and listened for the voice of God. When the lion and the bear did attack his sheep, David knew that God would strengthen him to defeat the enemy and protect his sheep. King Asa, his descendent, obviously inherited David's wisdom and courage.

3. Provision for Prosperity

The king, who serves under a king of kings, must not only consider the welfare of the people he rules over, but he must also work to increase the wealth and glory of that king of kings, who expects tribute money from each kingdom for his royal coffers. The king is the one who must supervise the expansion of business, agriculture and foreign trade for this dual purpose.

Therefore, the king has to be an industrious planner and negotiator. He needs to develop relationships with other kings and strike up trade agreements. The people need to be motivated to be bold and aggressive in creating business for trade with other nations. He must do whatever he can to increase the revenue of his people, which he can then tax to increase the revenue of the king of kings. If he does his job well, his people will be happier and more prosperous, and he will win greater favor with the king of kings making his own position more secure.

For us, as kings under our King of Kings, there are many applications of this truth. Many saints depend on our leadership to motivate them to step out and use their natural and spiritual gifts to build the Kingdom of God. Too many kings have had the Saul spirit and repressed the divine aspirations and destinies of those under their rule.

One of my favorite examples in leadership is Iris Ministries, led by Rolland and Heidi Baker. What an inspiration they have been to us and hundreds of thousands of people world-wide! Here are two leaders of an amazing revival in Mozambique, where miracles happen consistently and thousands of Muslims, in the previously unreached Makua tribe, have been converted in a very short time. Hundreds of churches have sprung up through the convincing power of God in the healing of deaf ears, blind eyes, crippled bodies and so much more.

But Heidi and Roland are such examples of the "David" spirit. They train pastors and missionaries by the hundreds every year, but totally release them to serve God wherever they feel called. There is no pressure to stay under their Iris covering. They build God's Kingdom and God keeps giving them more of their own kingdom to rule over and administrate.

As we mentioned in the first chapter, there is good news. The Saul spirit is dying, and through people like Roland and Heidi Baker, a new empowering spirit is being released in the church of Jesus Christ. The "David" kings are willing to empower the gifts of their people, and they are anointing them to go into every part of society to bring greater prosperity to their kingdom and thus to the Kingdom of God.

As previously mentioned, kings need to negotiate with other kings and open doors for trade and commerce. As kings under Jesus, we should work together with other leaders in the Kingdom and find ways that will bring blessings and prosperity in a win/win relationship to all concerned. We all prosper when we do this and the Kingdom of Heaven prospers with us.

In the next Chapter we will talk about being kings in the various mountains of society. But first let's look at the amazing privileges we have as kings under our King of Kings.

Privileges of Kings

Years ago, I received some insight on the ways of kings from the book of Samuel. In chapter eight, God tells Samuel that the people have rejected Him in asking for a king. However, He instructs Samuel to tell them exactly what a king will do. From this passage I gained insight and application regarding the rights and privileges of the King (Jesus) who rules over us.

Now, I also understand that as kings under a king of kings, there are privileges for us to accept, as long as we keep in mind the responsibilities we have already enunciated. First, let's look at the passage that records the words of Samuel to the people:

This will be the behavior of the king who will reign over you. He will take your sons and appoint them for his own chariots and to be his horsemen, and some will run before his chariots. He will appoint captains over his thousands and captains over his fifties, will set some to plow his ground and reap his harvest, and some to make his weapons of war and equipment for his chariots. He will take your daughters to be perfumers, cooks, and bakers.

And he will take the best of your fields, your vineyards, and your olive groves, and give them to his servants. He will take a tenth of your grain and your vintage, and give it to his officers and servants. And he will take your male servants, your female servants, your finest young men, and your donkeys, and put them to his work. He will take a tenth of your sheep. And you will be his servants. (I Samuel 8:11-17)

From the passage above, we can clearly see that kings, in order to fulfill their roles as rulers, have the privilege of using the resources of the people and their possessions. Twice the tenth (or tithe) is mentioned. The king also has the right to draft the best of the young men and women for his own service. It appears that the king may make any use of the resources of his nation that he desires.

Surely, this all applies to Jesus, our King of Kings, but how does this apply to those of us who have been raised up to be kings under Him? If we were to try to take such liberties with people in our churches or ministries, we would surely meet with a lot of opposition and desertion, especially in the western church. Is there any practical application we can make from this biblical model?

The answer is yes, but we certainly must understand things from a position of wisdom and grace. We need to understand how Jesus operated on the earth as a king. Jesus certainly fulfilled the responsibilities of a king, and He was also able to take advantage of the privileges of a king as well, even though He ended up being crucified by His subjects. However, the cross was just a necessary step Jesus had to take to ultimately receive the full authority and majesty of His Father's Kingdom. We can function as kings on the earth today by learning from His example.

King Jesus

The Apostle Paul so capably described the example of Jesus in Philippians 2:5-11. He exhorted us to have the same attitude mind-set as Jesus, Who had the right to remain in a place of equality with God in Heaven, but gave it up and humbled Himself to become a servant and die in humiliation as a common criminal.

How do the life and death of Jesus teach us to take our positions as kings on this earth? The secret is revealed in Philippians 2:9-11.

> *Therefore God also has highly exalted Him and given Him the name which is above every name, that at the name of Jesus every knee should bow, of those in heaven, and of those on earth, and of those under the earth, and that every tongue should confess that Jesus Christ is Lord, to the glory of God the Father.*

The first word, "therefore", is very significant. Although Jesus is our King of Kings and Lord of Lords, when He came to earth, He came as a servant to His Father. *His Father was, in essence, His King of Kings*, and verse 8 tells us that Jesus was obedient to His Father, even unto death.

Jesus was clearly teaching us by example how to be kings on the earth. He came to serve and to share the Good News of the Kingdom of Heaven on earth. His message to His subjects was that God was their King of Kings who would bring justice, protection and prosperity, and He (Jesus) was the King under His Father who would bring His Father's love and goodness to His subjects on earth. As the angels declared, "On earth peace, good will toward men!"

At the same time, Jesus moved in a great level of authority as a king under His Father. He commanded his disciples, "Follow Me!" He took authority over sickness, death, the elements and the laws of physics. He rebuked the unjust leaders and cleansed the temple of the money changers. He knew He was a king and walked in that authority, while at the same time He was the perfect Servant to His Father and to His Father's subjects.

This is how we are to then function as kings on the earth. We spend time with Jesus, our King, and learn his heart and mind regarding His people on earth. He then sends us to represent Him the way He represented His Father.

That means we humble ourselves and serve our subjects, standing up for those who are being treated unjustly, protecting those who are weak and needy and blessing the hungry with food from Heaven. We serve in humility, yet with great authority. We use the resources of those that God has given us to further the Kingdom of Heaven on the earth.

When we move in a kingly, apostolic anointing, demonstrating God's love and power to our people, they will respond to our prophetic and apostolic declarations, as the disciples did to Jesus. For instance, we may speak to another brother in a meeting and say, "Lay your hands on George and command the fever to go now, in the name of Jesus." Or we may say to a cripple, "Rise up and walk in the name of Jesus." Or like Peter, we may say to the dead person, "I say to you, 'Arise!'"

To put it more clearly, as kings under the King of Kings, we should be able to move like the apostles in the book of Acts. We should exercise all authority over all the forces of nature, the power of the enemy and the flesh of humanity. All of this comes out of intimacy with our King of Kings and the humility that is imparted to us in His presence.

DECLARATIONS AND DECREES

One of the greatest privileges of kings is the right to make declarations and decrees that actually become the law of the land in a kingdom. Some of the examples we have in the Old

Testament are from emperors or kings of kings. Cyrus king of Persia made a decree that the Jews could return to their land after seventy years of captivity.

King Ahasuerus also made decrees regarding the Jews after Haman persuaded the king to have them destroyed. Later he made another decree allowing the Jews to defend themselves. Both of these decrees could not be changed once they were stamped with the king's signet ring.

King Darius of Babylon made a decree that no one could worship anyone but him, as a result of Daniel's enemies trying to have him destroyed. As we know, the king could not change his own word, so he had to throw Daniel into the lion's den. Fortunately for Daniel, his angels shut the mouths of the lions, and Daniel's enemies became fine dining for the hungry cats.

Other kings like Saul and Herod, who were not kings of kings, also had the power to make decrees. Saul declared that anyone who ate food on a certain day of battle must die, and it was only the intervention of the people that spared his son, Jonathan, from death. Herod, who was under the Roman Caesar, decreed that all male children, two years and under, should be killed.

As kings, we should take this authority seriously and use it when we know it would bless and please our King of Kings. There are times when we need to use this authority to take territory the enemy has stolen from the people of God. We can proclaim that Jesus is Lord over a city or nation. We can decree that His Spirit will minister in dreams and visions to the unsaved on our street and to the members of our own family who are not walking with God.

As we look at the mountains of society in the next chapter, we can apply this truth to assist us in taking control where the enemy has been entrenched in days gone by. We must come to realize that we are kings and we do have this authority. The devil knows it, but we are still not too convinced in the body of Christ. The Holy Spirit is moving upon us in these days to make us aware of who we are and how to walk with God with the right heart and attitude.

WALKING WORTHY OF OUR HIGH CALLING

In Ephesians 4, before Paul discusses the five-fold ministries of apostles, prophets, evangelists, pastors and teachers, he makes the following appeal:

I, therefore, the prisoner of the Lord, beseech you to walk worthy of the calling with which you were called, with all lowliness and gentleness, with longsuffering, bearing with one another in love, endeavoring to keep the unity of the Spirit in the bond of peace. (Eph. 4:1-3)

The call to function as a king is a certainly a high calling. Paul makes it clear here, as in so many other passages, that we walk worthy of a high calling by getting low. As servants under authority, we are positioned with authority that comes from above, and we can serve with the power and authority of Heaven to demonstrate that the Kingdom of Heaven has come to earth.

SOME INSIGHTS FROM JESUS' TEACHING

Jesus told a very interesting parable related to kings and kingdoms that Luke recorded for us. The story begins like this:

A certain nobleman went into a far country to receive for himself
a kingdom and to return. (Luke 19:12)

We don't need to get into the intended application of this passage. Rather we want to use this passage to reveal what the people in Jesus' time already understood. It is simply a fact that kingdoms were "received" by someone with royal blood, and they had to go to a far country to receive it. This verse clearly reinforces the point that we made earlier that kings and kingdoms, as they were known by the people of Jesus' day, were granted by a higher king – a king of kings.

Obviously in those days, the nobleman would go to Rome, make himself available as a faithful servant of the emperor, and he would be given the authorization to rule and reign over the nation he was from. When he returned, he would be proclaimed king of his kingdom and would have the documentation to prove it, signed by the king of kings.

Jesus continues the parable saying that the nobleman gave money to ten of his servants to invest for him. When he returned, most had invested and multiplied their money for him. The first one had invested one mina, and it had earned ten minas. Jesus responded, *"Well done, good servant; because you were faithful in a very little, have authority over ten cities."* (Luke 19:17)

This story gives a clear understanding of the structure of kings under kings. In those days the ruler of a city was often called a king. Therefore, the king over a country could have city kings under him, just as he was under the greater king of kings. This is like a king raising several sons and dividing his kingdom under them.

Another familiar passage is Matthew 16:19.

And I will give you the keys of the kingdom of heaven, and whatever you bind on earth will be bound in heaven, and whatever you loose on earth will be loosed in heaven.

This passage is another strong support for the fact that God gives us a kingdom to rule over. The keys of the kingdom of heaven are from the King of Heaven, and He gives us authority on earth to function as kings with the backing of the Kingdom of Heaven.

Chapter Three

King of the Mountain

*M*any children have played the game, King of the Mountain. In war, armies endeavor to conquer the hilltop and gain the advantage over the enemy who has to climb uphill to attack. Those on top of the mountain clearly have the advantage, but climbing to the top is not so easy when others are there before us. The top of the mountain is a very small place. There is no room for a lot of people at the top, as there is at the lower levels of the mountain.

One of the dominant themes in apostolic and prophetic streams is the theme of the seven mountains of society. The basic thesis is that these seven mountains have been taken over by non-Christian or anti-Christian forces, and God is stirring His people to rise up and conquer these mountains for the Kingdom of Heaven. We believe God wants to expand His Kingdom and bring in His harvest. This will become much easier when the enemy is not in control of media, education, government, etc. We will instead be able to make a huge impact with a positive influence on society.

These mountains are:

1. Family
2. Religion
3. Government
4. Media, Communication
5. Arts, Entertainment
6. Education, Science, Medicine
7. Business, Finance

If we look at each of these mountains in detail, it is clear that they have been conquered by those who do not love or submit to our King of Kings. For instance, what is going on with the Family Mountain? The amount of family strife, rampant divorce, gay marriage activism and brutal abortions all are signs that we need some godly leaders or Christian kings at the top of this mountain.

On the mountain of religion, we see growth of Islam, Eastern Religions, New Age and occultism, along with the extreme liberalization in Protestant Christianity. We may be making progress in our own little stream, but we are not taking the proper leadership to influence this mountain of society.

In each of the mountains, we can see how anti-Christ forces have been at work. In the government mountain, for instance, the church has been far too silent for far too long. We have allowed anti-Christian representatives to control our legislative and executive branches, which in turn have appointed an ungodly judicial branch.

In media, the secular news networks have long controlled the way we get our news, deciding what is and what is not news. We know that over 90% of news outlets are controlled by liberals who usually pretend or profess to be neutral in their communications.

In the arts and entertainment, we have let godless people control Hollywood because we thought TV and movies were immoral. We've been fighting to regain our footing, but we are currently at a very low place on this mountain.

Education was taken over by humanists, who made a concerted effort to infiltrate the teaching universities in America about a century ago. This has been a key target for them because all these bright, young people will be impacted. No matter which mountain they spend their future on, the mountain of education will be their base.

As for the business and finance mountain, Christians have felt for too long that money itself was evil and shouldn't be pursued. The end result is that we have left the business and finance mountain to godless, as well as greedy, people. There are incredible opportunities available to serve God and help bring in the harvest. There are also thousands of willing workers, but there is not enough money to send them. God wants that to change.

WRONG FOCUS

The prevailing mindset in the church for centuries, coming out of the dark ages, is focused on whether we are good enough for God. Will we make it to Heaven or not? Is our salvation secure or can it be taken away from us if we backslide? The entire focus has not been on God's Kingdom, but on our own personal salvation. Consequently, we want to avoid anything that would make us look like the world with its evil and greed.

For instance, my parents kept me from anything that sounded worldly to them. That included all dancing, movies, tobacco and alcohol, with the exception of a Christian film and maybe two very innocent movies during my childhood.

However, God is changing our focus significantly today. We have found that if we become more intimate with God, He gives us great assurance of His love and our salvation. God is able to download His desires to us, and we begin to think like He thinks. If He wants to rule the business and finance mountain through us, we can go after that mountain with zeal and enthusiasm. We know that we are doing it for His Kingdom's sake, and we don't have to fear it costing us our eternal home in Heaven.

Christians need to realize that they have been called to be kings representing the King of Kings rather than just subjects of this world. We must find out which mountain(s) God would have us influence and then go as high as He allows us to go. However, we must always remember the example that Jesus set forth and the responsibilities of kings, which were discussed in the previous chapter.

BECOMING EQUIPPED TO CLIMB YOUR MOUNTAIN

One of the most important messages in this book is that God wants you to be a mountain climber. But mountain climbers must be prepared for the multitude of challenges that face every brave man or woman who says to God, "Give me this Mountain!"

If you decide to become a mountain climber, you will need to develop *special skills* through special fitness training that you wouldn't need if you stayed in the comfortable valley. You will have to be prepared for unusual weather, such as sudden storms, including blizzards and very low temperatures. The higher you climb, the thinner the air, and the more difficult it will be to breath.

Before you climb your mountain you will need some *special equipment*. You will need boots that can grip the ground and dig into the ice at the higher levels, lightweight protective clothing to keep you from freezing to death, and some tools like picks and ropes. You will also need a carefully filled backpack with high-energy nutritious food, along with enough water to get to the level where you will be melting snow to drink.

In addition, you must learn to work with a team. You must learn to trust others with your life, and you must be willing to be trustworthy for others as well. The bigger the mountain, the more you will need the team to get to the top.

But probably the most important item in the mountain climber's arsenal is not his training, his equipment or his team, but his passion, courage and determination. Without these inner-character qualities, the average climber will quit when the going gets too tough, often letting down others who are depending on him.

To climb our mountain, we must have a strong inner conviction that we can and we must fulfill our destiny by not quitting until we reach our prescribed place on that mountain. We must know that God has made it possible, and He will help us reach that position on this mountain.

Mountains Under Enemy Control

The insights shared above deal with simply climbing mountains that are not controlled by the enemy, but now let's add the element of war. The mountain may not be as high as what typical mountain climbers ascend, but even a modest hill that is under the control of an enemy army, which is fully equipped with cruel and deadly weapons of warfare, will require more preparation, great courage and unflinching endurance.

In varying degrees, all seven mountains today are under the rule of the enemy of our souls, who is also the enemy of Jesus Christ. These are mountains that we can and must conquer for the love of our Lord and Master, our King of kings.

This puts a little different slant on the idea of being a king. Instead of the mental picture of a king on his throne, who is surrounded with luxury and many servants to do his bidding, we are now looking at a picture of a soldier in camouflage gear, who is joining forces with others, as they prepare to engage the enemy in deadly warfare, even to the point of hand-to-hand combat. We might want to think twice about the cost of becoming a king in God's Kingdom.

But how can we say "no" to our King when He has given us the opportunity to rule and reign with Him? We know He is with us, and He has given us power and authority over all the power of the enemy. The battle may be fierce for a time, but we know that we win. We can't lose when we listen to His voice and get His instructions.

Every mountain of society has a group of kings under their own king of kings, who is the prince of the power of the air. They rule for him and for their own lust and greed.

The family mountain in our society is ruled by forces that believe that marriage is optional, children are often undesirable and disposable, homosexual relationships are normal, and men are usually self-centered wimps. Organizations such as Planned

Parenthood receive taxpayer dollars to promote some, if not all, of these beliefs and practices. Advocates for the gay agenda are ready to fight anyone who has the nerve to disapprove of their chosen self-destructive lifestyle. The war is raging, but few Christians want to tackle the family mountain and take the flack that will come their way if they should try to bring it under God's control.

The religion mountain is greatly divided with various kings in varying degrees of unity and warfare with each other. Strong religious spirits keep people in bondage to religion and a false concept of holiness. Humanistic philosophies and liberal theology have also invaded many traditional denominations, teaching that the Bible is full of myths and man is the center of everything. Multitudes of non-Christian religions, including witchcraft, have also taken root in America and other western nations, and anyone who takes a stand in a public forum, proclaiming the present power of our supernatural God, is attacked by all the power of the media mountain kings.

Speaking of the media mountain, there is no doubt who has been in control in the western world. We know that a small elite group of multi-millionaires or billionaires control the masses by the news that they do or don't choose to publish. What they do publish has a liberal slant and spin.

We know that a steady diet of the regular media will shape the way we think, transforming our minds a little by little with slanted views. The introduction of Fox News to the mix was a step in the right direction, but we need some strong kings to conquer this tremendously important mountain.

When it comes to government, there are many battles ahead of us before we can claim control of this mountain. As we are beginning to see, the government system is full of greed and corruption. A few strong leaders have been able to position themselves at various places on this mountain, but the vast majority of the leaders in high places are not ruling on behalf of the King of Kings. They are in the grip of the enemy of our souls and will often do his bidding.

We don't need to say much about the arts/entertainment mountain. Since the invention of moving pictures and the television, movies and TV programs have stooped to new moral lows almost every year. We have seen some brave Christian soldiers attacking this mountain with some good quality productions, but there is a long way to go to the top. We need to prepare the troops for this tough battle.

Our friend, Shawn Bolz, has established a base on this mountain in Los Angeles, California. He has met and ministered prophetically to many famous and influential people in the movie industry. He is also inspiring many others to take their proper place on this mountain and bring the change that is needed.

Atheistic education and evolutionary science have a stronghold on the education mountain. To move them off the top of the mountain will be a huge battle, but as with the others, we can win the battle for this mountain with the help of our Commander-in-Chief. Humanists targeted this mountain a century or more ago and have worked hard to take it away from Bible-believing Christians. For the sake of future generations, it is a must that we conquer and hold this mountain.

Finally, the business and finance mountain must be taken for God. Because of the warnings about greed and forgetting God in times of prosperity, the church has found a safe haven in living poor and humble. With little vision for the Kingdom of God and the fulfillment of the King's desires, the church has focused on its own holiness rather than intimacy with the God of holiness.

To accomplish the goals of Heaven on earth, we must mature enough to handle the dangers of prosperity and wealth. This is very strong on God's heart, and it's for this reason that thousands of prayer houses with hundreds of thousands of saints seeking intimacy with God are being raised up. Many of these will be given resources far beyond what is considered normal to do great exploits for God. The resources will come from kings on the business and finance mountain.

Like any other king, a king on this mountain must be prepared and equipped to handle the battle and win. This coveted mountain is already covered with the blood of those who have battled with each other for supremacy. We, the kings who represent the King of Kings, must know God's strategy for taking this mountain His way. His ways are not man's ways, and we will conquer them with His wonderful wisdom.

God's Perspective

It should be clear that we need a paradigm shift when it comes to being kings with Jesus. Being a king is not about living in luxury, and it should not be an option. It is a calling from God of service and humility, of warfare and prayer. God in His wisdom has chosen to "need" us to take our place as kings, in order for Him to fulfill His role as King of Kings over all the earth.

In the next chapter, we will examine the relationships of kings in the Kingdom under the King of Kings. Who is in charge and who is to serve whom? You might find it very interesting. Following that we will discover the manner in which kings receive their royal inheritance.

Finally, we will share an exciting prophetic word about anointing kings to bring change and reformation to the world as we know it. This book is in part a result of that message, which was shared in a conference. After the message was publically released, it was suggested that it should be made into a book. Thanks Jess for your kind encouragement.

CHAPTER FOUR

PLAY YOUR POSITION

*T*he most frequent exhortation of a kids' soccer coach is, "Play your position!" Playing our position in the Kingdom is far more important than playing our position in a soccer game.

What normally happens when kids play soccer? Everyone typically gravitates toward the ball. No one wants to stay on the opposite side of the field and wait for a pass. The fact is that a pass will almost never come because there are so many players surrounding the ball that there is little hope that it will get very far from the middle of the cluster. So why not jump in where the action is and see if you can get your foot on the ball and move it a foot or two in the right direction.

Does that sound a little bit like church today? We all want a piece of the action, wherever that seems to be in our particular church world. It seems nobody is ever going to pass the ball to us, so we might as well fight for it like everyone else. To get the ball, we not only have to fight the other team – the enemy – but we also have to compete with the players on our own team to get a piece of the action.

But from the near sidelines, our loving Coach is shouting,

"Play your positions!" He knows that's the only way we can score a goal and reap the benefits together. We must play as a team or we will surely lose.

American football is another sport where playing your position is extremely important. Each player has an assignment for each play and his failure to perform that assignment will usually mean a broken, failed play. Players have different skills and physical size and strength. Some are huge and seemingly overweight, while others are built for speed and agility. There are special teams with specific assignments. Kickers get paid to come out on the field a few times each game for a few moments, but their job is important enough to command a huge salary.

So it is in the Kingdom of God. Each king under the King of Kings is like a high-priced football player on a professional team. He must know his position and play it well. He must be willing to sacrifice his body and endure some pain and discomfort for the sake of the team.

Each player is very important to the team and they must know that. Every teammate playing with them is also very important, and they must honor them and their skills and allow them to play their positions without interfering or being jealous of the attention they get.

Many players on the team get very little attention compared to the few who actually handle the ball. For the team to succeed, these players must be content to know that they are just as important as any other player, even though they don't get the attention that they may deserve. Their joy comes when the play succeeds and when the game is won.

This is a very critical point for Kingdom positioning. Many kings will serve in more obscure places, having been positioned by the King of Kings where they are needed most, but not necessarily where they will get the most attention. They may face great challenges and difficulties fulfilling their assignments, but they may be the only one with the right skills and capabilities to do a great job where they have been planted.

Playing Our Position on Our Mountain

Some people are gifted and trained in many areas and can be positioned where they are needed most, like a utility player in baseball. But most people have more specialized training and gifts and are much more effective if they are placed in the proper position in the Kingdom.

Let's combine the mountain analogy with the football team analogy. If we have an opponent controlling the mountain, and his position is well-entrenched at the top, it will require all of us working together as an army/team under the leadership of our Commander-in-Chief/Coach. We must have special forces/special teams for certain operations, as well as regular ground troops/offensive team, covered by air support/pass protection.

I trust you get the point. We are not well-advised to independently approach the bottom of the hill and shout at those on the top that we are kings and want to rule the mountain. We might just find some rocks or boulders heading our way, with a little help from those who presently control the mountain. Each mountain must be conquered, and if we don't get our acts together and become an effective team, with each member fulfilling his or her own purpose and destiny, that will not happen.

If we truly want to please God and expand His Kingdom, we must all lay down our personal ambition for glory and honor and develop a passion for seeing the King of Kings exalted and honored. That exaltation and honor increases every time we take more of our mountain. That's why it is so important to develop a spirit of unity. Without unity, we can't take any mountain, and without taking the mountain, God won't receive the honor and glory He deserves.

ROYAL RELATIONSHIPS

On every mountain, there must be many kings with varying degrees of authority. The potential for "border clashes" and "sibling rivalries" is huge, but is also extremely dangerous to our holy cause. How can we as kings, all serving under the same King of Kings, prevent this harmful behavior from happening?

We may find ourselves positioned on the mountain within the sight of another king who has very strong opinions. In fact, he may have a very strong opinion about his very strong opinions. The problem is that we might also have a very strong opinion that is in direct conflict with his very strong opinion.

If we are both kings and we must work together, who is the boss and who will decide whose opinion is correct in a given situation? Must we have a military-style chain-of-command to work out such issues? Within a denomination, or a particular apostolic network, those issues can be more easily resolved under a system of hierarchy.

However, we are now talking about the Kingdom of Heaven, which is not a denomination or a single apostolic movement. We are talking about the entire body of Christ learning to work together in the same level of unity that was exhibited by the early Jerusalem church. Is this just a "pipe dream", or is it reasonable to believe that God, who did it once before, can do it again for those who would be His representatives on this earth?

Today, can God give us the grace to work together in a loving relationship without the need of a judge and jury to decide who is right? Are there any suggestions in the Word of God about how we should handle such situations with each other in working relationships? Actually, the Bible is full of them.

One of the best verses in the Bible that teaches us how to work with other kings on the mountain is I Peter 5:5. Perhaps the numbers give us a clue. The number 5 represents grace. The book's author, Peter, has five letters. It's the fifth chapter and the fifth verse. The verse even ends up talking about grace. Let's see what it says.

Likewise you younger people, submit yourselves to your elders. Yes, all of you be submissive to one another, and be clothed with humility, for God resists the proud, but gives grace to the humble." (I Peter 5:5)

Yes, whether we like it or not, the prescription for getting along on the mountain is humility. Learning to have a submissive spirit, when we think we are right and the other king is wrong, is crucial to the advancement of the Kingdom of Heaven on our earthly mountain.

As a general principle, the younger kings should willingly submit to the wisdom of those with greater experience in serving the King of Kings. But the over-riding principle is that even the older and wiser kings should be clothed in humility and very willing to listen to the appeals of the younger, passionate kings.

God will often test us older and wiser kings by giving secrets to the young bucks and hiding them from us. Will we pull rank and reject their ideas, or will we have the wisdom to listen and discern if God has actually spoken to them? The way we respond will reveal to us and others if we have a "Saul" spirit or a "David" spirit. Remember, the Saul spirit has to die, but the David spirit will rise up and conquer.

God's grace will be the deciding factor in who controls the mountains. Without God's grace, we cannot take our mountain. Grace is our secret weapon and it gives us the "unfair advantage" that we need since our enemy is already on top of the mountain. Taking it from him is harder than defending it, because the one on top always has the advantage of gravity. You can shoot arrows and throw stones much farther downhill than you can uphill. We need the grace advantage and we can't have it without humility.

Because humility is the last thing that our flesh wants, I know there will be kings who have been positioned on the mountain for some time who will, sadly, fail this test. There will be "Davids" with great ideas that will be resisted because of spiritual pride. These kings will be surgically removed from the mountain by the King of Kings, Himself. The "Davids" will not touch these kings; they will put them in God's hands and humbly wait for their time.

ROYAL ALIGNMENTS

The time has come for kings in the Kingdom to understand their alignment assignment. God is joining his leaders together in a manner that is not the norm in ecclesiastical circles. The government in God's Kingdom is a government in which leaders honor and prefer one another above themselves. It is a government in which all leaders have the capacity to converse directly with their Commander-in-Chief, enabling them to work together in complete unity.

Even so, royal alignments are important for the practical functioning of the government of God on the earth in our generation. We must become familiar with the unique gifting and personalities of those with whom we are called to work. Just as the players on any sports team need to get familiar with the moves and skills of their teammates, so kings in the Kingdom need to know the people they work with.

It will be necessary for us to work with those who are stationed in close proximity to us on our mountain. We need to know what assignments they can best handle themselves and which assignments we should take responsibility for ourselves. The important thing is that each job gets done in the most effective and efficient way possible. The goal is always to gain more and more control of the mountain for our King of kings and not to expand our own little kingdom at the expense of our neighboring king.

How do we actually discover and fulfill our alignment assignment? There is no secret formula, but there are definitely some good guidelines to follow.

ALIGNMENT GUIDELINES

1. Who do we already know that is on the same mountain with the same heart for the Kingdom?
2. Who has already inspired us and/or received inspiration from us?
3. When we meet other strong Kingdom leaders, is

there a "kindred spirit" that draws our spirit to them?

4. Whose character and anointing combine to best compliment our own?

5. Does the Holy Spirit witness to our spirit that we can trust them?

6. Are they in humble alignment with other leaders?

7. Are we willing to let God overrule our own desires if He asks us to align with some we don't really like?

God's alignments will continue to shift as we move into positions of more and more domination on each mountain. He will continually raise up new kings to work with us. Some will move very quickly up the mountain and by-pass those of us who have been on the mountain for a great length of time. We must honor these latecomers as God's anointed leaders and resist the temptation to be jealous and hinder their upward progress.

Every king positioned under the King of Kings has received their position and commission from God, and we need to be at peace with God's decisions. But let's take a quick look at how this process works in the Kingdom of Heaven on earth and how we get prepared for the kingly assignment from our King of Kings. These simple truths will help us function in our strategic alignment.

Chapter Five

Training for Reigning

Kingdom Inheritances

Revelation 1:6 tells us that Jesus has made us to be kings unto God, but how does He actually do this? It is obvious that people cannot just decide to become the king and have everyone serve them. There is a normal process and protocol that must be followed before anyone is recognized as the king.

From Father to Son

Every kingdom had to begin with its first king. Obviously, the first king did not come into the kingdom by being a prince first. In other situations, a monarchy line can come to an end and has to be replaced by a new royal family. However, as we all know, the normal pattern of any kingdom is for the eldest son of the passing monarch to take the throne and wear the crown of his father. The Kingdom is inherited, just like houses and lands and personal possessions.

One great advantage of this tradition is stability in the kingdom. The subjects of the king know that the royal family will continue to be the royal family, which provides continuity in the kingdom, especially when the king is perceived as a good or benevolent monarch. Consequently, when the changeover takes place, the people can look forward to the coronation celebration with the hope that the reign of the son will bring positive changes to the kingdom.

Whereas elections can tend to temporarily divide a country, coronations tend to unite the country. There is an element of honor or even worship that normally accompanies the office of the king. As we know, people were created to worship, and the human representative of the unseen omnipotent and eternal Being is often the king the people set over themselves. The common cry of the people is, "Long live the king!" As a human being, they know that the king won't live forever, but they always wish him long life, which is indicative of their tendency to worship their king.

Another tremendous advantage to this tradition is that the prince is trained from birth by the king himself for this very important destiny. No one is better equipped to prepare and train up a future king than the present king.

This is good news for every Christian. We all have the same Father, and He is the ultimate King of Kings. If we allow Him, He will take the time with us to prepare us for the privilege and responsibility of ruling and reigning with Him.

Our advantage is that as we serve under our King, He does not have to die before we are given a throne and a crown. He died before we ever knew Him that we might become kings. He is our King of Kings and we serve as kings under His absolute authority. The blessing of this arrangement is that our mentor is always there for us. We never have to make decisions totally on our own. We exist to bless Him and His glorious Kingdom, and He dearly loves to bless us and our specific kingdom because we are His sons. As Jesus said, *"The Father loves the Son and shows him all things that He, Himself does."* (John 5:20)

The Father not only loves us, but because He loves us, He shows us everything that He does. Therefore, if we walk with Him as sons of the King, He will teach us and prepare us for our royal destiny.

As we look back at our history of walking with God, we may see things a little differently when we realize that God has been preparing and training us to rule and reign. Any good teacher or mentor does not only show us how to do things, he or she lets us try to do it ourselves. Many of the challenges that we have faced have been orchestrated by God to give us the chance to walk through situations the way that He would.

Remember that Jesus came as a human and faced many of the same challenges that we face. He was tempted, tested and tried by fire. He was coached and mentored by His Father, and He came through every challenge victorious. We have the same Heavenly Father, and the more time we spend with Him, the more He reveals of Himself, which allow us to handle every challenge and every trial according to His grace and mercy.

Training Courses in the Father's School of Kings

1. People Skills

Rulers in any kingdom will always have to work with people, and these people may have a wide variety of personalities and cultural backgrounds. The king must relate to all of the people in his kingdom, not just the royal family. He must be able to relate to the poor and the uncultured, as well as to the wealthy and the sophisticated.

Inner Healing

Those who want to occupy the throne provided by their Heavenly Father should take this training course seriously. Too many leaders unnecessarily wound their people through a lack of wisdom and grace, simply because they have never learned to place value on people and their individual personality makeup.

The biggest problem is that every person has experienced personal wounding in the process of growing up. These woundings can cause significant problems when dealing with other people. Certain words or actions can trigger irrational responses, because they bring subconscious flashbacks to earlier hurts and wounds.

The good news is that there are many ministries now focusing on this great need in the Kingdom of God. Most of our own family have received personal healing ministry, which is sometimes called "inner healing" or "deliverance". This ministry and the knowledge and training that can come with it give us, as believers, the tools to combat the emotional and mental attacks on our minds and hearts.

Our own ministry team has devoted much time and energy to make this a priority for those who want to work with us. We believe that most problems in team ministry come from people who are hurting and not completely healed. If they learn to identify their pain and the reasons for their offensive actions and reactions, they will be better equipped to work in a spirit of unity.

Without this healing in our inner being, we find ourselves doing harm to the kingdom that has been entrusted to us. We offend people by our anger, impatience, rudeness, bitterness, moral failures, greed, fears and insecurities. We can see many of these issues in people like King Saul and other kings of Israel, as well as in many spiritual leaders of our time. Some of these spiritual leaders have self-destructed and have been removed from their high position, often by secular courts.

The most dominant reason why our fleshly weakness overcomes our desire to be like Jesus is the fact that we have been hurt and wounded, and we have roots of bitterness that need to be pulled out of our hearts and minds. These roots open the door for demonic powers to build strongholds within us, and we lose some of our freedom to make wise choices.

We find ourselves reacting in ways that we know are wrong. We say things and do things that we have to apologize for, and many of those responses become habitual and control our lives. Without pulling out the roots and planting godly seeds in their places, we cannot be trusted with too much power and authority as kings.

Spiritual Fruit and Godly Character

The fruit of the Holy Spirit listed in Galatians 5:22-23, is basically a list of godly people skills and character qualities. Love, joy and peace for instance are attitudes that attract people, making them feel valued, fulfilled and safe. Longsuffering, kindness and goodness are needed in a variety of situations to bring healing and reconciliation. Faithfulness, gentleness and self-control keep our subjects loyal and peaceful.

All of these Spiritual Fruit reduce discontentment, resentment, anger and warfare. These are the spiritual seeds that replace the ungodly roots that produce the pain and hurt in those we love and work with.

This wonderful Fruit of the Holy Spirit is hindered from taking root when the tares sown by the enemy have already taken root in our soul. However, when we root out the tares, and let the Holy Spirit produce the positive fruit, we begin to develop positive character traits.

For instance, when we work with someone who is having a bad day and makes a slightly rude remark, we can choose to respond out of our pain, making things worse, or we can respond with understanding, love and grace from a healthy heart. The soft answer will usually turn away wrath and disperse the cloud of atmospheric tension. When we repeatedly respond in a correct manner, it becomes a positive, subconscious habit. When it repeatedly produces positive results, then right responses will become second nature.

The reason that the Fruit of the Holy Spirit works so well is because it is a product of the Spirit of the Father and of the Son. The Holy Spirit working through us is the Father teaching and mentoring us. When we listen to the voice of the Holy Spirit, we are being shown by the Father what He does. It is the same Holy Spirit that ruled the heart and mind of Jesus, the Son of Man, on the earth. He was giving us on-the-job training for reigning and schooling for ruling.

2. Ministry Gifts and Callings

God always gives spiritual gifts to His kings and queens to

give them an "unfair advantage" over the enemy. This is especially important when we consider the fact that we are trying to displace our enemy from his perch at the top of the mountain we are trying to conquer. With equal fire power, the army at the top should always be able to repel the army below. Given superior fire power, the army at the bottom can force the enemy to relinquish his grip on that mountain.

Superior Intelligence

First of all, spiritual gifts give us superior "intelligence" for warfare. The gifts of knowledge and the discerning of spirits give us secret information about the enemy. The king of Syria discovered that fact when Elisha continually told the King of Israel the details of Syria's battle plans. (II Kings 6:8-23) The enemy does not have the same information about God's plans and cannot anticipate our actions and strategy, giving us that wonderful "unfair advantage".

Superior Recruiting Capabilities

Secondly, we have the gift of prophecy, which can be used in many ways. The gift of prophecy is a recruiting tool for enlisting new soldiers in the army of God. Jesus used this gift repeatedly in John 1 to recruit his own disciples, including Peter, Philip and Nathaniel. We use prophecy to give people a glimpse of their purpose and destiny, which gives them understanding of their importance in the Kingdom and their value to the King of Kings. The appeal to both the young and older generations is difficult to resist.

Superior Redeployment of Injured Soldiers

Prophecy is also used to encourage soldiers that are wounded and discouraged. When enemy soldiers are wounded, they are discarded and left to die. However, when a Christian soldier is wounded, the prophetic gifts are there to heal his wounds, raise him up and get him back into the battle. When prophetic ministry is fulfilling its purpose, Kingdom armies sustain very few casualties. Without prophecy functioning properly, we lose our soldiers left and right.

The Christian landscape today is littered with casualties of war. Multitudes of Christians have left the organized church, still believing in God, but not able to get along with other believers, especially those in leadership. They have hurts and wounds, and they don't know how to deal with them. In most cases, no one is there to bring them prophetic encouragement and get them back into the battle.

These wounded soldiers almost always believe some kind of a lie from the devil about themselves and everyone else they are involved with. They accept shame, self-pity, guilt and condemnation. They believe they have no hope, no value and no purpose for living. They continue to exist, they hope they are still saved, but they drop out of the quest for conquest and certainly don't have the mentality of a king ruling and reigning with Christ.

Prophetic ministry can do two things for wounded soldiers (through the gift of prophetic knowledge). It convinces them that God knows and really loves them; He forgives them, plans great things for them and has the power to restore them. We have seen prophetic ministry function this way hundreds and thousands of times. We have seen dozens of suicidal people find hope and purpose and then return to serving God.

Two other gifts that can bring about the same results are tongues and the interpretation of tongues. The person who prays in tongues is encouraging himself in the Lord. Interpreting a "message in tongues" (which is different than praying in tongues), encourages others and has the same effect as a prophetic word, according to I Corinthians 14.

Superior Strategic Battle Plans

Through the gift of Wisdom, which often defies common sense, we have a distinct "unfair advantage" over the strategy of human or demonic minds. When the Father reveals His strategy, it carries a surprise element that always catches the enemy off guard. I can quickly recall many biblical battles where God directed leaders like Joshua, David, Asa, Jehoshaphat and others to do things that made little sense. There was no way that the residents of Jericho could plan a defense against the unconventional battle plans that God gave to Joshua.

The gift of wisdom gets very little attention, as it seems less spectacular than the gift of knowledge or prophecy. The gift of wisdom is the strongest gift of the apostle and is certainly one of the most important gifts that kings rely on. James told us that if we lacked wisdom, we should ask for it. (James 1:5) He was not talking specifically about the "gift" of wisdom, but I believe the same principle applies. The gift of wisdom is something that leaders should earnestly pray for.

Superior Power

The enemy has absolutely no power to compare with the power released through the gifts of faith, healing and miracles. When these gifts are in full operation, through kings with purified motives and healed wounds, we can march confidently up the mountain and conquer our enemies so quickly that they don't know what hit them.

Just look at the examples in the book of Acts. The first signs and prophetic declarations brought three thousand to Christ. Healings, deliverances and miracles brought thousands more into the Kingdom of Heaven very quickly. Acts 4:33 says, "And with great power the apostles gave witness to the resurrection of the Lord Jesus. And great grace was upon them all."

THE AMAZING POWER OF LOVE

Love was mentioned above as a Spiritual fruit, but it is so much more. Pure love coming from the heart of God for people is the most powerful weapon we have to overpower the enemy on whatever mountain we are on. We have seen amazing transformations take place through the raw power of supernatural love.

The story that made David Wilkerson famous is one of those examples. The power of love broke down the walls of hatred, anger and bitterness in the heart of Nikki Cruz and other gang leaders. Revival was soon taking place among the gangs of New York City and a new ministry called Teen Challenge was birthed.

A former Hamas youth leader, the son of one of the founders of the Hamas, became a Christian after much searching when he read the words of Jesus, Who said, "Love your enemies." He had never heard of such a concept before, and he experienced that love, as he turned his heart over to Jesus and became a part of the body of Christ.

JUSTICE AND MERCY

Another extremely important training course for kings is the course on justice and mercy. This is a course that the Father teaches us by example as we walk with Him. Because of the power and authority that goes with the position of king, even under the King of Kings, there is a temptation to use and abuse that power and authority in ways that do not please God.

We mentioned in a previous chapter that meting out justice is one of the most important responsibilities of a king. If we walk with God and ask Him for His wisdom in this area, He will teach us as a loving Father.

God is a God of justice and that requires sin to be dealt with. However, He declares that mercy triumphs over judgment (James 2:13), and as His delegated representatives, we must learn what that means. Learning when to overrule the need to execute negative justice with God's mercy is very important to a king.

Reading the Book of Psalms on a regular basis would be a wise thing for all of us kings to do. David and others who wrote the Psalms talked a lot about the mercy of God. The term, "tender mercies" is used eleven times in the Psalms (KJV). David also declared, "Your gentleness has made me great." (Psalm 18:35) David recognized that God was very merciful when He certainly had the right and reason to be harsh with him. He discovered instead that God was tender and gentle with him.

King David needed this perspective, and we, as kings, also need this perspective. We need to know God as loving, gentle and full of mercy.

FINANCIAL STEWARDSHIP

How a king handles kingdom resources reveals where his heart is. The young prince observes his father's spending and saving priorities and will usually follow in his father's footsteps. Money is the greatest source of political and social power and authority. In our society, it often determines the results of elections, appointments and personal favors.

It is clearly important for us to learn from our Heavenly Father and observe His ways with financial resources. Of course, God doesn't need money to run His Kingdom, but he interacts with us on earth, and His Kingdom on earth is always interacting with money and financial situations.

The early Jerusalem church, which was clearly the church under the most direct leading of the Holy Spirit, continually dealt with financial issues and is a good indicator of God's view of Kingdom finances. In Acts 3:6, Peter declared that he had no silver or gold, but he did have the power to heal the infirmity of a life-time cripple.

However, by Acts 4:34-37, we find an enormous flurry of financial activity, as people were selling property and possessions and laying the proceeds at the apostles' feet. From this point on, money was collected and distributed to care for the poor and to spread the gospel. Deacons were chosen to help solve financial issues, and later offerings were taken to help feed the church in Jerusalem, which was going through a time of drought.

A few things stand out about the way God, our King of Kings, handles Kingdom finances. First of all, He can still work miracles when resources are not available. He paid the temple tax with a miraculous fishing trip, when Peter found the coin in the fish's mouth.

Secondly, when God's power and love are being demonstrated through apostolic leaders, the finances begin to pour into the Kingdom coffers, supplying the kings with plenty of resources to expand the Kingdom borders. These financial resources are laid at the feet of trusted leaders who have demonstrated that God is in them and flowing through them.

Thirdly, there was incredible concern for the well-being of every member of the body of Christ. We read in Acts 4:34 that there was no one that lacked among them. The amazing generosity of the believers ensured that everyone's need was met. This clearly is the heart of our King. He loves his subjects and is always concerned about their well-being. As children of the King of Kings, we need to have the same heart and compassion that He does, and we need to rule our designated kingdom with the same financial principles.

As kings, we have access to incredible financial resources. In the coming transfer of wealth, this will become a reality for many of us. However, the responsibility as stewards of this wealth has been the ruin of many great Kingdom leaders in the past. Scripture clearly warns us about the dangers of mishandling money and loving or depending on it rather than God.

We cannot take these warnings lightly. James 3:16 says, "*For where envy and self-seeking exist, confusion and every evil thing are there.*" Self-seeking and envy almost always involve money. When we go after money with self-seeking motives, confusion and evil are with us, and we open the door for the enemy to destroy us.

On the other hand, if we share the Father's heart, we can do great and wonderful things with the resources that come through our hands. We can lift up and encourage those in financial bondage. We can finance the training and sending of harvesters and warriors to bless the Kingdom. We can feed the hungry and gain a platform for sharing the Good News of the Kingdom with multiplied millions of needy souls that God loves and desires in His royal palace.

We can also enjoy the personal blessings He wants us to have. God does not have a poverty mentality. He lives in a palace, His children are royalty, and they also belong in the palace with their Heavenly Father. He has no problem with His children having the best clothes to wear and enjoying the luxuries of the palace. He will bless them from time to time with the desires of their hearts, which will often involve financial resources.

As Paul wrote, *"I know how to be abased, and I know how to abound. Everywhere and in all things I have learned both to be full and to be hungry, both to abound and to suffer need."* (Philippians 4:12) Paul had found the balance of being able to enjoy prosperity, but also the ability to endure suffering for the sake of the Kingdom. In our training for reigning, God will usually allow us to experience both prosperity and suffering.

These scenarios will test us, and the prosperity test is probably the most difficult to pass. When we suffer loss or the danger of loss, we tend to cry out to our "Daddy God" and ask Him to help us. When the blessings and resources abound, we tend to forget how much we need Him and focus on what we can accomplish for ourselves with the resources in our hands.

This is the reason that God doesn't just supply every need and want immediately. He is training us carefully by not giving us more than we can handle. If we lose our intimacy with Him, all the resources He gives us will not serve His purposes, it will affect the fruit of our service to Him, and we will not be able to spread His fire to others because we won't have it to give away.

SENSE OF HUMOR

The longer you walk with Father God, the more you realize that He does have a sense of humor. Sometimes it appears that He likes practical jokes, as He teases you with crazy situations. Perhaps we should imitate Him sometimes to lighten the stress load. My wife dearly loves a painting that a Korean pastor gave to us. It shows Jesus with His head tilted backwards in laughter. The Bible tells us that God sits in the Heavens and laughs. (Psalm 2:4) Jesus told His disciples that He came to give them joy and wanted their joy to be full.

Another evidence of God's sense of humor is the way He often allows us to think that He is going to do something a certain way, in a certain period of time, but then He changes everything. Later we understand what God was saying and how we misinterpreted it. Biblical prophecies are often mysterious and difficult to understand. It seems that God delights in setting up treasure hunts with secret clues that only make sense after we discover the next clue. I'm sure God gets a chuckle when we think we have prophecy all figured out, when we are actually a long way from solving the mystery.

As kings in training, we must learn not to be so serious all of the time, as laughter has confirmed health benefits. The up-and-down action of laughter is very much like wholesome exercise. It causes the internal organs to function better, circulation is improved, and it helps the body remove waste, which helps the body ward off disease. I also recently learned that joy helps build and restore brain function from infancy on. We need to take time to enjoy God's creation and rest from our spiritual labors, as well as our physical labors. The Sabbath was God's idea, not man's idea. He made it for us, not for Himself.

I personally need to apply this truth more to my own life. I love to see things produced and accomplished. I love to see growth and progress. In one sense, that's where I get some of my joy. But I also need to learn to laugh with others and enjoy their company more.

The pressures of the Kingdom require emotional release. Many distinguished leaders have demonstrated a great sense of humor, which helped keep their sanity and ability to make wise decisions. President Ronald Reagan had a sense of humor that endeared him to the public, and it helped him handle the stress of his office.

What's Next?

We have been examining some of the vital courses in the "School of Kings". But how do we actually become a king with the authority and responsibility that goes with that position? In the next chapter, we will look at God's plan for placing kings on their thrones. It has to begin with the anointing process, but who will do the anointing and whom will they anoint? The next chapter is a prophetic word for the church of today.

CHAPTER SIX

THE ANOINTING OF KINGS

In the first chapter, we discussed the death of Saul and the anointing of King David. That anointing took place at God's command when Samuel, the senior prophet and priest of the nation of Israel, took a flask of anointing oil and poured it out on the young shepherd boy. In the first chapter, we shared a prophetic interpretation that the Saul spirit is dying and the David spirit is rising up to take its place.

In this chapter, we will look at another prophetic story and draw some very important conclusions that I am quite enthused about. Let's look at the story in II Kings 9. This story occurs several generations after King David. Israel has been divided into two kingdoms – Judah (with Benjamin) in the south and Israel (the other ten tribes) in the north. The northern kingdom of Israel was much more evil than Judah and had several very wicked kings.

The prophet Elijah confronted Ahab, king of Israel, and challenged the prophets of Baal on Mount Carmel. When Elijah left the earth in a whirlwind, his prophetic mantle and office was passed on to Elisha. Near the end of Elisha's life, Joram was king of Israel. The people were still following the ways of Ahab and Jezebel by serving Baal. God told Elisha that it was time for a reformation in the land. He instructed Elisha to anoint a new king, even though King Joram was still in power.

Let's read what Scripture tells us about this story and then see what God is speaking to us today through it.

And Elisha the prophet called one of the sons of the prophets, and said to him, "Get yourself ready, take this flask of oil in your hand, and go to Ramoth Gilead. Now when you arrive at that place, look there for Jehu the son of Jehoshaphat, the son of Nimshi, and go in and make him rise up from among his associates, and take him to an inner room.

Then take the flask of oil, and pour it on his head, and say, 'Thus says the Lord: "I have anointed you king over Israel."' Then open the door and flee, and do not delay."

So the young man, the servant of the prophet, went to Ramoth Gilead. And when he arrived, there were the captains of the army sitting; and he said, "I have a message for you, Commander." Jehu said, "For which one of us?" And he said, "For you, Commander."

Then he arose and went into the house. And he poured the oil on his head, and said to him, "Thus says the Lord God of Israel: 'I have anointed you king over the people of the Lord, over Israel. You shall strike down the house of Ahab your master, that I may avenge the blood of My servants the prophets, and the blood of all the servants of the Lord, at the hand of Jezebel. For the whole house of Ahab shall perish; and I will cut off from Ahab all the males in Israel, both bond and free." II Kings 9:1-8.

This story has many parallels with the original anointing

story that was shared in the first chapter. It also has some distinct differences, one of which we will focus on in this chapter. Let's look first at the similarities.

First of all, both of these stories involve the anointing of a new king while the old king was still in power. Both of the older kings were rejected by God, and both of the new kings were anointed to bring reformation to Israel.

Secondly, there were older prophets with great influence and authority in the nation. Samuel was highly respected and feared by the people as a seer, prophet and judge of Israel. He had anointed Saul and then David. Elisha was a prophet with a great miracle anointing, who carried the mantel of the great prophet Elijah.

Now let's look at the one extreme difference, which will launch us into the prophetic word for all of us in the Kingdom of Heaven on earth.

A MAJOR PARADIGM SHIFT

The biggest difference in these two stories is the fact that Elisha did not go himself to anoint Jehu – he sent a young man, a "son of the prophets". He is also called a "servant of the prophet." At first, this might not seem that unusual, but let's take a closer look at it.

Anointing a new king was one of the most important jobs that any prophet performed, and it was not very often that a new king was anointed. This was not your everyday prophetic ministry to the average person. The anointing oil you pour out on a king empowers that man to impose his will on an entire nation. This was a very important ceremony, and it was conducted by the most honored and most spiritual person in the nation.

It's like choosing a minister to pray an inaugural prayer when a president is put into office. You don't pick a part-time pastor of a church with fifteen members. You choose a Billy Graham or a Rick Warren. However, God used Elisha to make a statement, which Elisha was quite willing to make. In fact, he had made a somewhat similar decision once before.

Some time earlier, Naaman, a Syrian general, came to Elisha to be healed of his leprosy. Instead of honoring a foreign dignitary, Elisha sent out his servant to give him self-help instructions. It was an action that was so contrary to the normal protocol of the day that Naaman would have returned home in anger, had his servants not talked him into following Elisha's instructions.

Now Elisha probably didn't have a lot of sympathy for the Syrian general. Remember how Jonah was not willing to bless the Syrian capital of Nineveh? However, in this present situation, anointing a new king of Israel, you would think that Elisha would be more than willing to do the important and lofty task of taking the oil himself to Ramoth Gilead to anoint Jehu as the new king of Israel.

In my imagination I see a different picture:

God says, "Elisha, I need you to send one of your no-name sons of the prophets, one of your servants, to go and anoint Jehu as the new king of Israel. It's time to put an end to the worship of Baal, and Jehu is the man I have chosen to bring reformation to Israel."

Elisha responds, "God, am I hearing you correctly? Are you asking me to stay home and send a virtual kid in my place? Don't you think this is a job for a senior prophet? Why would you send an amateur for such an important assignment? Did you forget that I was given Elijah's mantle? Don't you remember that I saw him taken up and was given a double portion of his anointing? It would really make a much greater impression if I was the one anointing him."

"You heard me correctly," the voice from Heaven replied. "It's a new day Elisha. I want to make a statement. It's no longer a day for superstars. There will be many prophets following you, but none will have your reputation. Instead, I want to anoint many prophets, and I want to use the least known to do the greatest jobs. Can you understand what I am saying, Elisha?"

"Well, I'm trying. I do find it a little humbling, but you are my Boss and I will follow your instructions."

"Good. Here is what I want the young man to say ..."

A PROPHETIC PROCLAMATION

This is a day that God is shifting our ministry paradigm. This is a time in which God is going to use the younger generation to do amazing exploits for the Kingdom of Heaven on the earth. From the little children, to the youth, to the young adults, the anointing will be poured out on the militant, fearless and passionate warriors.

Older Christians, who are more passionate than the average church person today and don't want to be left out of the action, will work with the younger generation to provide some measure of stability and wisdom. They will be in the minority, not the majority. They will give up their rights of seniority willingly to allow the younger generation to flow in their own anointings and make their own decisions, as they listen to the voice of the Holy Spirit.

It's time to anoint the new warrior kings of the Kingdom. There will be many young prophets, and they will be anointing many young kings. God is not looking for seniority; He is looking for passionate worshipers who are not entangled in the affairs of this life. God has a harvest to reap, and an enemy to put to flight. God will use those who are fearless and ready for the challenge. The job requires too much reckless abandon to entrust it to those who might want to serve God, but have too much personal stuff to walk away from, like the rich young ruler in Jesus' day.

In the story of David, we saw how God chose a young man to be king. In the story of Jehu, we see how God chose an unnamed young man to be the prophet that anointed the new king. Saints of the Kingdom, it is now the time for the younger generation to rise up and do both the anointing and the reigning.

COMMANDERS ARE WAITING FOR THEIR ANOINTING

When the young prophet arrived in Ramoth Gilead, he found a group of military leaders just sitting around. Empowered by the authority and the affirmation of the man-of-God from the older generation, the servant of Elisha boldly spoke to the group and singled out Jehu, whom he called "commander".

Jehu represents a generation of worshipers/warriors who wonder what God has for them to do and when they will get their assignment. They have been filling the houses of prayer, fasting and interceding and worshiping by the hours. They have been soaking in the presence of God, getting visions and dreams and crying out to God for more of Himself.

This subculture of the Kingdom of Heaven on the earth has

been growing rapidly in the last few years. I have no statistics to prove it, but I have been observing this movement for some time, and there is no doubt that it is growing all over the world. It is made up not of senior citizens with lots of free time on their hands, but of young people looking for a cause to live and die for.

They are an army waiting for orders, but much more than that, they are kings, who don't know their royal calling. They want to serve God and lay their lives down for Him. They are willing to be "nobodies and nothings", but don't know they are also called to conquer and rule the mountains that God wants to give them. How are they going to fulfill their destiny, if they don't know what it really is?

I believe the biggest reason they don't know their destinies is because they have not been told that they are kings with an assignment from the King of Kings. They have not been taught that they are called to possess a mountain, and establish their own kingdom under Jesus, the King of Kings.

If that is the problem, then the solution seems obvious; we need to tell them. Pastors and apostles can teach them, and they can read books like this one. However, what can really convince them is the word of a prophet speaking directly into their personal destiny. It worked in a powerful way with Jehu, and it will work with today's young worshipers/warriors.

The prophet of God can quickly convince these young worshipers/warriors that God knows them, loves them and wants them to rule and reign with Him under His authority. The prophet can stir the passion and the longing in their hearts that God has put there in days gone by. He can activate gifts and callings that have been semi-dormant, waiting for the prophetic word to fan the flame within their hearts.

CALLING ALL PROPHETS

It seems to me, however, that we have a shortage of prophetic people to take the flasks of oil to anoint the new kings. What is the problem and what is the solution?

The problem is that we have depended on a few professional, highly gifted prophets to do all the prophesying, and there just are not enough of them to go around. Most of them get burned out and withdraw from the personal prophetic ministry. They may prophesy over a few people called out of a crowd, but very few even do that in these days.

What we lack is what Elijah and Elisha had – the School of the Prophets. We desperately need older prophets to mentor and raise up a multitude of younger prophets.

We need to empower them before they have "earned" their stripes through long-time service. The older prophets need to empower them by transferring their anointing like Moses did with the seventy elders. They must then trust the young men and women that they have trained and empowered, and they need to let them do the "big stuff" in the Kingdom. They will do a better job than we expect.

In fact, the danger is that the older generation might feel threatened by their strong anointing. The temptation is to feel that we, as the older prophets, are not needed any more. Then we can either quit or we can become territorial and jealous, like King Saul.

The solution is to keep recruiting more young prophets to father and to empower. In II Kings 2:12, when Elijah was being taken up in a whirlwind, Elisha cried out, "My father, my father!" Elisha was the young prophet then, but he had been fathered by Elijah. Fathers are always needed and honored by the younger leaders.

Fathering involves loving, empowering and rejoicing in the exploits of the children. A normal father would never be jealous of his son's success, because he feels like he is also successful when his son succeeds. Only a very insecure, unhealed father will fight his son's success.

A Sad Truth

One of the problems we face in the Kingdom of Heaven on the earth is the fact that personal financial survival and success takes priority over the expansion of God's Kingdom. Prophetic ministries and evangelists of all kinds usually have to raise their own support. They seldom partake of the tithes of the saints, which go to local churches to pay salaries of various pastors and to maintain facilities and programs. I explored this subject in greater detail in my book entitled, *Folding Five Ministries into One Powerful Team*.

At any rate, usually only the most charismatic personalities and most gifted para-church ministries can survive. Some do quite well, but many quit trying because they can't raise enough money to pay their bills. The prophets that do have successful traveling ministries usually cannot afford to mentor a younger generation of prophets. There are very few ongoing schools of the prophets in western Christianity.

The result is that we have a shortage of young prophets to anoint the young warriors. The solution to this problem is three fold.

First of all, we need to educate the body of Christ and teach them the importance of raising up the kings that will rule with

Christ. We then need to teach them the need for prophetic ministry to empower and anoint those kings.

Secondly, we need the existing prophets to focus more on transferring their anointing to the young Elisha's in their lives. They need to see the importance of multiplying their anointing in others. Then they need to give them assignments from the Lord, including the more important ones. This effort will require more faith for financial provision, but if God is in it, He will provide miraculously and greatly reward such obedience.

Thirdly, we need to all value one another as important players in the game. God has called us all to be kings. He has commanded all of us to desire earnestly to prophesy. He also told us to walk worthy of our calling by being humble, honoring one another and by guarding the unity so the thief cannot steal it from us. We need to recognize that in God's economy, He often chooses the weak, the foolish and the "nothings" to surprise the strong, the wise and the "somethings" of this world. We need to honor the ones He honors and not despise their youth or their lack of standing in the ecclesiastical hierarchy.

I think most Christians have felt the sting of rejection when approaching a well-known minister. Granted, most big-name ministers are bombarded with people wanting to tell them something or wanting special prayer or the opportunity to pray or prophesy over them. They often develop a resistance to such people and often do not have a lot of grace with people they don't know.

At the same time, I know that there are times when the famous speaker just plain feels that the person wanting to talk to them is beneath them and has nothing important to say. Too much power and praise of man tends to create an arrogant spirit, and most Christians have been wounded by such a spirit and don't know how to handle it. They often tend towards bitterness and remove themselves from active duty.

This is one reason God has chosen to use a multitude of non-famous under-aged carriers of the glory and power of God, rather than a handful of puffed up superstars in the Kingdom. When people don't put you up on a huge pedestal, they won't be so easily offended if you let them down. If a young person gives you a word that doesn't make sense to you, it is easily brushed off with the thought, "I know he meant well, but he's still learning and just missed it."

On the other hand, if a well-known prophet implies something on the negative side, or tells you to marry someone you don't agree with, it can really throw you off your game. The more honor we are given, the more dangerous we become if we get out of the anointing and move in our own flesh.

A few years ago we met a lady who had received a prophetic word from a very well-known prophet that she should marry a certain man. The man turned out to be a homosexual, and she went through hell on earth before getting a divorce from him.

By the same token, if a famous prophet gets it right and releases God's power to do miracles, we tend to give honor to the prophet more than to God. When a young unknown Kingdom warrior gives an accurate word and releases God's healing power, we tend to give the glory more to God, because we know that this vessel is a "nobody", and it had to be God.

I think it's quite clear that God is shifting our paradigm and causing us to become the generation of harvesters where we all are kings, we all prophesy and we all do our part to bring in the harvest. To do so, we need to establish God's Kingdom on the mountains of society to impact and influence the whole world with the love and the power that Jesus, the King of Kings, has given to his children on this earth.

At this point, I believe it's time to tie up some loose ends and try to make as much sense as possible of the insights and revelations we have downloaded in this book. May God help us all to have the appropriate responses to the wisdom and knowledge that He gives us in this aspect of our Christian walk and service in His amazing Kingdom.

CHAPTER SEVEN

YES, YOUNG LADY, YOUNG MAN — HE'S TALKING TO YOU!

Is God really telling you that you are called to be a king or queen and rule over a kingdom of your own? Yes, He is talking to you, not the other guy or gal! He really needs you to rise up and sit on that throne to bring justice, protection and prosperity to His subjects under your influence.

One morning, I was getting ready to go to an early meeting where Brenda and I would be speaking. I opened my Bible to spend a little time in meditation. My eyes immediately fell on one of the many passages that declare that God resists the proud, but gives grace to the humble.

The Holy Spirit made a strong statement to me at that very moment. He said that God was really looking for those with enough humility, so that He could exalt them to positions of honor and authority. He had many positions to fill, but there was a shortage of people who qualified to be trusted with such honor. He was not looking for power or talent or charisma – He was looking for humility. That revelation made a strong impression on me, and I have shared it many times.

Are we willing to pay the simple price for honor? Are we willing to humble ourselves under the mighty hand of God? Kingdoms are available. Are we going to apply for the position?

Important Definitions

It seems contrary to the purpose to define the most important terms at the end of the book instead of at the beginning. But I felt it was necessary to let the book evolve naturally, and by the time we came to the final chapter, we would have a more clear and comprehensive definition of our important terms.

A. King

The practical definition of "king" is simply, "*One who has received the responsibility and the authority to rule over a region, an entity and/or a people group.*"

In the Kingdom of God, we have received the title of "king" from our Father, the King of Kings.

B. Kingdom

The practical definition of "kingdom" is "*A region, entity and/or a people group under the rule of a king.*"

In the Kingdom of God, our kingdoms are composed of people and other entities, also under the rule of Jesus, the King of Kings.

As kings in the Kingdom of God, we may rule over a physical region or territory, a business, a sport, a TV network or station, a family, a church, mission or ministry, etc.

Starting Where We Are

We don't have to wait until we have a Billy Graham ministry or resources to buy Walmart or Disney Studios to rule and reign with Christ. We can start where we are and we can start now.

Focus first on fulfilling the responsibilities of a king. If you are a father or mother, a big sister or brother, a teacher or just one in a group that hangs out together, you can begin to see those in your world as objects of your Father's love.

Remember, Jesus is the King of Kings over all the people in your life. Ask Him if you can serve them and be His instrument to provide them with justice, protection and prosperity. Ask God to let you fulfill the duties of a king to them.

Don't even begin to worry about the privileges or rights of a king. If you serve others like a king by bringing them justice, protection and opportunity for prosperity, you will eventually receive the honor as well, although that cannot be your motive. Your passionate desire must be to bless the King of Kings by bringing others to a place of dedication and commitment to Him so that they will serve Him with all their hearts, their talents and their gifts.

If God has given you a position of greater authority as a manager or business owner or pastor, use your position in the same way. Let it be your kingdom assignment from your Father, the King of Kings. Administrate your little kingdom the way that God would administrate it Himself.

Walk worthy of that calling as prescribed in Ephesians 4:1-3, with all lowliness and meekness, guarding the unity of the Spirit. Don't look at the people as your servants, but as those you serve. Let God's love flow through you to bring them healing, value and a strong relationship with your King of Kings.

Ask God for More

Jesus promised us that if we were faithful in a little, he would give us more. He told parables declaring that those who wisely used or invested their few talents would be given more talents or money. Tell God what you desire to accomplish as a king under His authority. Tell Him how you want to expand His Kingdom by enlarging your own.

This may mean asking Him to open doors for expansion and growth. It may mean asking Him to help you purchase a new business or corporation. It may mean running for political office or writing a radical, revolutionary book.

It may mean adopting a child, opening a day care or raising support for an orphanage overseas. It may mean training for an Olympic event or coaching a Little League team. It may mean trying out for a play or movie, entering a talent contest or even a beauty pageant.

Ask God for wisdom to keep your health and energy levels high. Don't allow burn-out, lethargy or disease to set in because of lack of self-discipline, laziness or gluttony. Eat healthy, exercise and get enough sleep.

Don't Limit Yourself

Remember that Jesus gave His disciples amazing promises. He said that they would do the same things and greater than He had done. He talked about moving mountains and cursing fig trees. He declared us to be the salt of the earth and the light of the world, just like Him.

We often limit God with our minds. We have listened to

other voices more than His. These voices tell us we are limited by our past sins, our race, our intelligence or apparent lack of it, our financial position, our personality and other factors. We often tend to believe the negative before we believe the positive.

But God says that we can do all things through Christ. He says that He has chosen the weak and foolish things to astound the strong and wise. He chose David, the only son of Jesse not considered worthy to be king.

Putting it bluntly, *"You have no excuse."* When you have reached a certain position on the mountain, look up higher and ask God to take you there. It's not only your privilege, it's your responsibility. Remember, you are not taking it for yourself, but you are building God's Kingdom by possessing it for Him.

Fathering More Kings – The Multiplication Process

As we grow the Kingdom of Heaven by taking our responsibilities as kings under the King of Kings, we can begin to multiply His Kingdom domain by training and raising up other kings. When we are functioning as kings and queens, we can bring other princes and princesses into the palace for training for reigning. We should get just as excited about them possessing their kingdoms as we are about us possessing ours.

Multiplication is an exciting phenomenon. Even if children only do 50% of what we do in our lives, ten children will produce five times what we did. But if we do a great job training them, and they produce double the results that we do, our ministry is multiplied twenty times. If each of us raised up one hundred kings and queens that each accomplished ten times what we did, our ministry is multiplied by one thousand.

This illustrates how important it is for the Kingdom of Heaven that we don't just focus on our own ministry. We need to focus on raising up other ministries as quickly as we can. Many of us can touch tens or hundreds of thousands of potential kings and queens. Some will touch millions in their lifetimes.

When we impact the multitudes to rise up and take the personal thrones that God has given them, we are bringing incredible increase to the King of Kings that we serve. What an honor and privilege. The rewards in Heaven will be huge. Even if we had none of the benefits of royalty on this earth, we will be so incredibly compensated in the life to come, which is coming so very quickly.

Potential Problems and Pitfalls

It would be great if everyone reading this book had pure hearts, clean hands and no pain from the past to mess up their emotional health and motives. But most of you reading this have experienced life as it is in this sin-cursed world, and most of you have been wounded and have learned to compensate in fleshly ways. The enemy has come in and in subtle ways affected the way you look at people and God as well.

Almost every Christian can use some personal ministry to learn how to forgive and grow in grace after being wounded by rejection, accusation, abandonment, shame and abuse, etc. These wounds hinder us from freely serving as servant-kings and queens in the Kingdom of God.

I would sincerely suggest that the reader find someone with some training in learning how to forgive and get healed in the soul. When we rule with an attitude that God didn't give us, we can hurt instead of help people. It has been so very aptly said that, "Hurt people hurt people." It is very important that we get as healed as possible before we infect other people with seeds of bitterness, accusation, fear and many other contagious diseases of the soul.

A spirit of pride can do great damage on the mountain where we are positioned. Pride is the number one reason for division. God desires us all to be one, not just doing our own thing, but working together for the Kingdom. We all have a life-long battle to kill pride and walk in true humility. If we say we have no pride we are deceiving ourselves in a big way.

INTIMACY – THE GREATEST PITFALL PROTECTION STRATEGY

If you could purchase insurance against spiritual pitfalls, you would want to buy the brand that focused on intimacy with God. During our times in His presence, He will heal us and surgically remove some of the pain and the pride of the flesh. Brenda and I have personally experienced the power of His divine scalpel. Will power cannot do what intimacy with God can.

"All ministry flows from intimacy", according to our beloved friend, Heidi Baker. I would add that the purest ministry flows from the deepest levels of intimacy as well.

OUR GREATEST REWARD

I believe our greatest reward will be the privilege of doing the same things the twenty-four elders did in Revelation 4:10. When they bowed down before Jesus and worshipped Him, they cast their crowns before the throne. If we have not taken our place as kings under our King of Kings, we may not have a crown to cast at His feet, as He sits on His throne. If that was the only reason to rise up to our calling as kings, it would be worth it. He deserves the crowns He has given us, but we have the privilege of appearing before Him and laying our crowns down at His feet.

THE NEXT STEP

The next step is "Look up". From where you are, what is the next opportunity on the way up the mountain? Don't look down to see what's below you, in case you slip downhill. Put that out of your mind. It's onward and upward for you as a child of the King, destined to rule and reign with Him.

Get a vision of yourself a little higher on your mountain and ask God for wisdom, grace and strategy to serve and bless your way to more influence, impact and opportunity to expand the Kingdom of Heaven on the earth.

Begin to spend more time in intimacy and prayer for God's highest purpose for your life to be fulfilled. Ask Him how you can best build His Kingdom. Ask Him for compassion for people, power over sickness and disease and for authority over all the negative attacks messing with your present environment.

Declare and decree, like a king would do, that the will of God shall be done in all the circumstances that affect your kingdom. Activate all of your spiritual gifts and the gifts of others on your team, and encourage all the other kings in your neighborhood. Have a victory mentality and don't let the devil push you around. Remember that God has given you an unfair advantage. Use it for His glory.

Finally, realize that you might mess up and slip when you get caught off guard. Get back up quickly and dust yourself off. It would be helpful to reread this book again before too long and then every so often to keep your focus. Feel free to share this book with others, and ask them to pray for you as you pray for them. As you work together with others towards the same goals, you will grow more quickly and take more ground for the King of Kings. He will then give you more ground.

Remember that because your Father is the King of Kings, you are a king or a queen by virtue of the fact that you are His son or daughter. Rise up and possess your kingdom. He has bequeathed it to you. Don't let it just sit there growing weeds. Go rule and reign and cultivate the coming harvest. You can do it. It's your destiny and it's your very life. Amen!

P. S. An Amazing Quote from Bill Johnson

"Royalty is my identity, Servanthood is my assignment. Intimacy with God is my life source. So, before God, I'm an intimate. Before people, I'm a servant. Before the powers of hell, I'm a ruler, with no tolerance for their influence. Wisdom knows which role to fulfill at the proper time." (From *Dreaming with God*, page 88)

Ben R. Peters

With over 40 years of ministry experience, Ben Peters with his wife, Brenda, have been called to an international apostolic ministry of equipping and activating others. As founders and directors of Open Heart Ministries, Ben and Brenda have ministered to tens of thousands with teaching and prophetic ministry. The result is that many have been saved, healed, delivered and activated into powerful ministries of their own.

Ben has been given significant insights for the body of Christ and has written fourteen books in the past ten years, since beginning a full-time itinerant ministry. His passions and insights include unity in the body of Christ, accessing the glory of God, five-fold team ministry, prophetic ministry, and signs and wonders for the world-wide harvest.

Open Heart Ministries
15648 Bombay Blvd.
S. Beloit, IL 61080

www.ohmint.org
benrpeters@juno.com

Holy Passion: Desire on Fire
Igniting the Torch of Godly Passion
by Ben R. Peters

Available from Open Heart Ministries
www.ohmint.org

With Me
A Captivating Journey Into Intimacy
by Ben R. Peters

Available from Open Heart Ministries
www.ohmint.org

Resurrection!
A Manual for Raising the Dead
by Ben R. Peters

Available from Open Heart Ministries
www.ohmint.org

PROPHETIC MINISTRY
Strategic Key to the Harvest

Ben R. Peters

Prophetic Ministry
Strategic Key to the Harvest
by Ben R. Peters

Available from Open Heart Ministries
www.ohmint.org

EXPLORING THE POWER OF THE MIRACULOUS TO BRING PEOPLE TO CHRIST

Signs and Wonders
TO SEEK OR NOT TO SEEK

BEN PETERS
FOREWORD BY BILL HAMON

Signs and Wonders
To Seek or Not to Seek
by Ben R. Peters

Available from Open Heart Ministries
www.ohmint.org

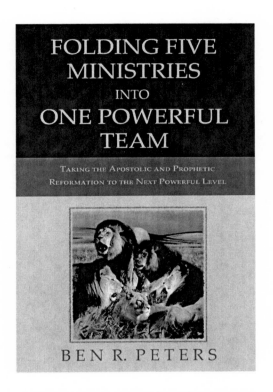

Folding Five Ministries Into
One Powerful Team
Taking the Apostolic and Prophetic Reformation
to the Next Powerful Level
by Ben R. Peters

Available from Open Heart Ministries
www.ohmint.org

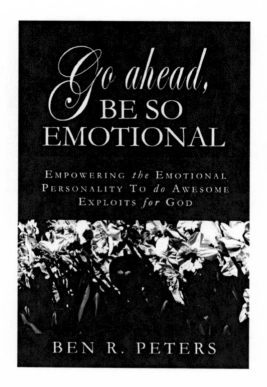

Go Ahead, Be So Emotional
Empowering the Emotional Personality
to do Awesome Exploits for God
by Ben R. Peters

Available from Open Heart Ministries
www.ohmint.org

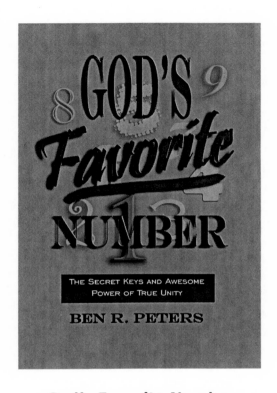

God's Favorite Number
The Secret Keys and Awesome
Power of True Unity
by Ben R. Peters

Available from Open Heart Ministries
www.ohmint.org

Catching up to the Third World
Seven Indispensable Keys
To EXPLOSIVE Revival
in the Western Church
by Ben R. Peters

Available from Open Heart Ministries
www.ohmint.org

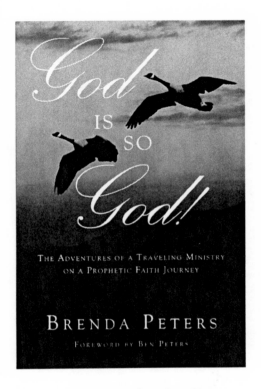

God Is So God!
The Adventures of a Traveling Ministry
on a Prophetic Faith Journey
by Brenda Peters

Available from Open Heart Ministries
www.ohmint.org

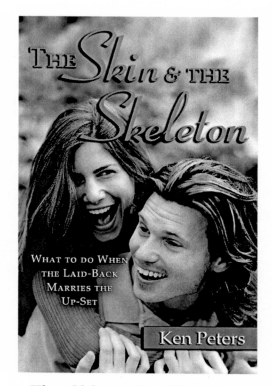

The Skin & the Skeleton
What to Do When the Laid-Back
Marries the Up-Set
by Ken Peters

Available from Open Heart Ministries
www.ohmint.org

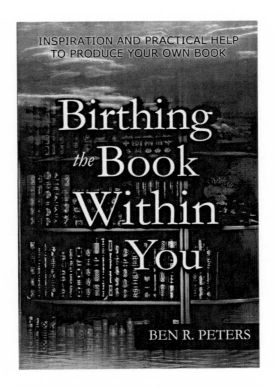

INSPIRATION AND PRACTICAL HELP
TO PRODUCE YOUR OWN BOOK

Birthing *the* Book Within You

BEN R. PETERS

Birthing the Book Within You
Inspiration and Practical Help
to Produce Your Own Book
by Ben R. Peters

Available from Open Heart Ministries
www.ohmint.org

Printed in the United States
145503LV00001B/4/P